Cinema and
Film's Challenge to Theology

Studies in Religion and Culture Series

Cinema and Sentiment
Film's Challenge to Theology

Clive Marsh

PATERNOSTER

First published in 2004 by Paternoster Press

09 08 07 06 05 04   7 6 5 4 3 2 1

Paternoster Press is an imprint of Authentic Media,
9 Holdom Avenue, Bletchley, Milton Keynes, MK1 1QR, UK
and
P.O. Box 1047, Waynesboro, GA 30830-2047, USA

Website: www.authenticmedia.co.uk

British Library Cataloguing in Publication Data
A catalogue record for this book is available from the British Library

ISBN 1-84227-274-8

Cover Design by FourNineZero
Typeset by WestKey Ltd, Falmouth, Cornwall
Print Management by Adare Carwin
Printed and Bound in Denmark by Norhaven Paperback

Contents

Studies in Religion and Culture
Series Preface

Perhaps more than ever before, there is a need for Christians to understand the shifting sands of religion and culture. Unfortunately it is with some justification that the church has been criticised, by both insiders and outsiders, for failing to understand the deep social, religious, and cultural changes taking place. This major series invites scholars to provide sensitive, empathetic, reliable, and accessible studies that will advance thinking about important subjects such as fundamentalism, mysticism, globalization, postmodernism, secularization, the religious significance of contemporary film, art, music, literature, information technologies, youth culture, religious pluralism, the changes taking place in contemporary world religions, and the emergence of new, influential, and alternative forms of spirituality. Whilst the majority of the contributors will be Christian thinkers writing with the needs of Christian community in mind, the series will be of interest to all those concerned with contemporary religion and culture.

Christopher Partridge

Introduction

This book explores what films do to people and what people do with films. It is a study of the role that films can and do play within the emerging and developing value- and belief-systems of people in the West today. Its focus is the location of film-watching and cinema-going within current patterns of living. In particular, the book explores the religion-like habit of cinema-going, and thus examines the religious function of film in contemporary Western culture.

The book recognises that there are both passive and active elements in film-watching. Something happens, or can happen, to people who watch films because of how films work, because of where they are watched, and who they are watched with. And all viewers bring to a film life-experience, immediate concerns, and worldviews. Viewers are not simply passive recipients of whatever 'message' a film may be deemed to convey. Exploration of this interplay between film and viewer is central to this study.

The two sides to the exploration cannot, though, be equal. In the first case, I can more easily draw on a wide range of responses to film, and delve into many disciplines of study, to gain access to some extent to 'what films do to people'. Here, the focus is inevitably on the interaction between a film and people who happen to have published responses, either theirs or a distillation of others'. Getting at what films do to people in a more incidental, informal way is much more difficult. This spills over into the second side of the exploration: what people do with film. Viewers may not, of course, consciously *do* anything with films at all: they simply enjoy them. In teasing out the two sides of the exploration, however, I shall demonstrate one of the ways in which the active 'use' of film works and why it is so important.

All film-watching happens within a cultural context. I make reference to the many dimensions of the contemporary Western context throughout the book. My specific concern is with *the contemporary theological significance of film* within that broader cultural setting. In other words, working out of a British context, I want to know how the religion-like function of film contributes to the shaping of viewers' lives. I am also keen to know what films are doing in relation to certain theological ideas, regardless of whether viewers consciously watch films with this interest in mind.

The book builds on, but marks a significant departure from, earlier work. In 1997 I co-edited with Gaye Ortiz a collection of studies *Explorations in Theology and Film*. It was a first of its kind on the British scene, and signalled a different approach from much of what had gone under the name of 'theology and film'. Many such studies, though speaking of theology and being largely Christian in origin, had depended on a 'universal theology' approach more in keeping with a religious studies perspective on the study of film than with a specifically Christian theological interest. They wanted to find universally valid theological themes, or hints of the transcendent, in the world of film as a way of pointing out the relevance of what religions already knew. Some of the studies in *Explorations in Theology and Film* moved close to that perspective too. With hindsight some essays veered too close to the 'illustrative' use of film, of which I was critical in one of my own contributions to the volume.[1] By contrast, it had been hoped to make the collection more demonstrative of the 'contributive' use of film, according to which film became a genuine resource with which contemporary Christian theology could work.

Less than a decade later, I find myself wanting to maintain the theological method proposed in that collection, together with the value of the worked examples I contributed, but to approach the whole question from a rather different angle. Were I to rewrite the methodological chapter – 'Film and Theologies of Culture' – in a literary context beyond that of an academic textbook for undergraduates, and a living context of further postmodern, social fragmentation and rapid technological advance, I would want to work with more nuanced definitions of the concept of 'culture'. In this present work, I shall reach questions of theological methodology quite late (Chapter 6). The main purpose of my dual exploration – what films do to people, what people do with film – is to examine what is actually happening, and to reflect theologically on this.

The book comprises seven chapters and four case-studies. I urge readers to work through the book in the order presented even though the book's two strands are not brought together until Chapter 7. Chapters 1 to 4 lay out the evidence of functions that

---

[1] C. Marsh, 'Film and Theologies of Culture' in C. Marsh and G. Ortiz (eds.), *Explorations in Theology and Film*, 31.

films and film-watching actually appear to be having in Western culture. Chapters 5 and 6 conduct the theoretical and methodological tasks of teasing out what should be concluded from such evidence. Chapter 7 draws out practical suggestions from the enquiry.

A number of people have helped bring this book about. Chris Partridge first suggested that I write it. I am grateful to Paternoster Press for including it in this series. Charlotte Haines, Ken Howcroft, Ian Maher, Ruth Nason and Ulrike Vollmer all read the bulk of the manuscript in draft form. Their critical observations and insights about both form and content have been invaluable. Any stylistic infelicities which remain are sure to have been added after Ruth worked on the text. I am particularly grateful to those of my readers who undertook the task of reading despite disagreeing fundamentally with some of my views!

Steve Nolan kindly provided useful material at short notice. Ian Bradley's interest in musicals seems to run in tandem with my own in film. I have enjoyed our e-mail exchange and look forward to seeing in due course – via his forthcoming *You've Got to Have a Dream: The Theology of the Musical* (SCM Press) – where each of our different enquiries might help the other. Finally, I thank my immediate family. Our children, Philip and Hannah, are sometimes bemused by the stuff I get up to. This book has encroached more than others on our communal life (the laptop has made it onto the kitchen table). I am grateful to them and to Jill for their understanding and patience.

1

Cinema-Going as Religious Practice

The Habit of Cinema-Going

A visit to the cinema is not simply a visit to see a film. For the most regular cinema-goers ('I go every Friday or Saturday night') a cinema visit may be a part of their 'life structure', along with working, eating, sleeping, shopping and relating to family and friends. Such a pattern of living may not be articulated as such, and may not be as neat as a person might wish, but it will exist in some form. As a major component (binding commitment) in a person's life, then, cinema-going is functioning as a religious practice for some. The regular, rhythmic habit of cinema-visiting contributes to the shaping of concrete living.

A second potentially religious aspect of the cinema-going habit is the acknowledgement of a need for rest and relaxation. It is not at all puzzling that religions receive a bad press for being killjoys, because very often they have been. Versions of Christianity throughout its history have been negative about dancing, card-playing and the theatre, for example. It is puzzling in the extreme, however, that religions have not been able to turn their respect for the need for relaxation into an appropriate lens through which to 'read' the world of entertainment. When people go to the cinema, whatever else they are doing, they go to enjoy themselves. Only those employed to be film critics, or to lecture or write on something to do with films, watch films for a job. Most people go for fun, to enjoy an alternative to the world of work; to 'escape' whatever fills much of their time. Like most contemporary entertainment, the practice of cinema-going functions as a form of 'sabbath rest' for people who need a break.[1] Whatever else films may do to and for

---

[1] Deriving from the Jewish Sabbath tradition, 'Sabbath' being the seventh day of the week, on which no work was to be done. Adopted in a variety of forms by Christian groups (most of whom, from earliest Christian times, celebrated the first of each period of seven days, Sunday, in celebration of the resurrection of Jesus Christ), the Sabbath tradition in Christianity went

people, it is not primarily for education, moral uplift, or spiritual nourishment that people are cinema-goers. The quest for relaxation may get tangled up with all sorts of other desires: to be scared, excited, titillated, or simply to have somewhere to go with a friend. But most are going to enjoy themselves.

Large numbers of cinema-goers (most?) go with friends.[2] However, whether people arrive in groups or individually, watching a film in a cinema is a shared experience. Cinema-going is therefore religion-like in being an experience enjoyed in the company of others. Excellent films can keep people enthralled even in video form, when watched on a standard-sized television in a living room. This experience is happening even more since the arrival of 'home cinema' technology packages. Even so, large-screen cinemas and cinema theatres create a different kind of experience again.[3] You may not know who you are sitting next to, but laughter, gasps of shock or surprise, and shed tears are infectious in a large group. As Martin Scorsese has commented: '... I can ... see great similarities between a church and a movie-house. Both are places for people to come together and share a common experience'.[4]

A fourth religion-type feature of the cinema is related to architecture. A number of contemporary buildings vie for the right to be termed 'today's cathedrals'. Shopping centres and multiplexes are high on the list.[5] Multiplexes attached to shopping centres are

---

[1] *(continued)* in two distinct directions: either accentuating the prohibition aspect, or encouraging the opportunity for recreation. Here I am stressing the latter, and in effect drawing on a 'Sabbath principle' within human living, without claiming any association with a particular day of the week. I do, however, note that a weekly cinema-going habit would inevitably continue a practice of structured recreation on a seven-day cycle.

[2] The exception to this may be the late afternoon/early evening times in large cities when individuals are found watching a film between work and home, sometimes as a 'chilling out' time. In some respects, cinema has perhaps here taken over a function more recently occupied by TV.

[3] B. Plate, 'Religion/Literature/Film: Towards a Religious Visuality of Film', in *Literature and Theology* 12 (1998), 26–8.

[4] Scorsese made the remark at the end of his TV/video documentary *The Century of Cinema: A Personal Journey* 1996; cited opposite the frontispiece of C. Marsh and G. Ortiz (eds.), *Explorations in Theology and Film*.

[5] Alongside sports stadia, I suggest. Ironically, medieval and modern cathedrals are recovering a clear sense of identity and purpose in the present, not least through being places which can bring together people from very different walks of life and a wide geographical region to explore their spirituality in relation to Christianity, sometimes quite anonymously. But they remain primarily historical buildings in the minds of many. The

arguably their 'chapels', whether or not they actually have a chapel.[6] As 'cathedrals' in their own right, multiplexes offer their own form of communion. They bring people together from far and wide, but dispense a common food.[7] They offer a wide choice of side-chapels (small theatres) alongside one or two main sanctuaries (large screens). They have trading posts in addition to the popcorn dispenser, where icons (posters of film stars) and 'texts' (biographies of saints/stars, videos, DVDs, screenplays) may be bought.[8]

The parallel between a multiplex and a cathedral may appear to break down, of course, when the precise meaning of 'cathedral' is explored: a multiplex contains no throne ('cathedra') for anyone like a bishop. But I am not so sure. The identification of 'cathedral-like' structures in today's world merely demands the parallel identification of whose voice is being deemed authoritative in Western culture. When the malls and multiplexes become the cultural equivalent of cathedrals, who is sitting on the throne? Critics of the whole exercise I am undertaking might cry 'Mammon' in both cases, as a way of observing the consumerist society in which we live. Again, though, things are not so simple. If cinemas and multiplexes in any sense participate in religion-like activity in Western culture, then film directors, (and producers, editors, and screenplay writers) or the film critics who shape our patterns of film-consumption may be functioning more authoritatively or at least more influentially than bishops. Such an observation highlights both the complexity and fragmentation of patterns of authority in a post-Christendom culture.

Attending a cinema 'religiously', then, i.e. as a regular, binding commitment, brings the cinema-goer into a range of practices

---

[5] (*continued*) buildings which *function* in the way that cathedrals once did in the medieval period are certainly shopping malls. This is not meant to imply, of course, that cathedrals were built for a commercial purpose; they obviously were not. But they did function as centres at which commercial transactions took place. I am most grateful to Geoff Sharpe for discussion on this point.

[6] As shopping centres sometimes do. Even if they do not have chapels, they increasingly have chaplains.

[7] R. Butler in 'A Night at the Pictures in 1994', in *Independent on Sunday*, 16 December 1994 wrote: '... (P)opcorn, Coke, hot dogs, ice-cream. They're the heart of the multiplex business ... The concessions stand runs right round the gleaming central tower ... The tower is to the foyer what the altar is to a cathedral'; cited in C. Marsh, 'Did You Say "Grace"?: Eating in Community in *Babette's Feast*', in Marsh and Ortiz (eds.), *Explorations*, 207.

[8] On 'Celebrity and Religion' see e.g. C. Rojek, *Celebrity*, esp. his telling comment on celebrities as 'part of the culture of distraction'.

which structure life, provide relaxing space, and create a shared experience for which cinema buildings are carefully designed.[9] For those who attend the cinema less often, individual visits may take on huge significance as 'special occasions' even though there is no reason to think that the watching of films more generally (on TV, video or DVD) has no place in their lives. If cinema-going is a particularly important form of film-watching, it is not the only way in which film takes on cultural significance. It merely accentuates aspects of contemporary living touched on in the more general practice of film-watching. These observations about the 'religion-like' quality of cinema-going do, however, press the point about a range of activities in contemporary Western life which may have taken the place of religion.

Three sets of questions arise. First, is cinema/film especially significant in this regard? Is it any more significant than watching TV or playing or watching sport, for example? Second, is there any particular value in identifying such cinema-going habits as akin to religion? And, what understanding of 'religion' do you need to have to be even able to do this? Third, where does this leave religion as more traditionally understood?

Is Film a Special Case?

Not everyone watches films. There are even counter-cultural people in the West who, by choice, do not own televisions. Most people do, though, watch a film at some stage, even if they do not go to the cinema very much. Even so, watching films is only one of a range of activities currently competing for the sociologists' attention as 'substitute religions' or 'alternatives to religion'. The 'secularisation thesis' suggests that Western culture has gradually becomes less and less dependent on, and therefore more detached from, religion. People simply do not believe in God or gods any more, it is said. Society functions therefore without reference to religion. Explicitly religious people become fewer and fewer and their religious activities become increasingly more privatised.[10]

---

[9] Late on in the research and writing for this present work I discovered M. Jancovich and L. Faire *The Place of the Audience: Cultural Geographies of Film Consumption*, a fascinating study of the development of cinemas in Britain, using Nottingham as a case-study. Though it will not be possible to refer extensively to ways in which their work is relevant to this present enquiry, I note here simply the many points at which the communal function of cinema is highlighted in their study, as well as fluctuations in the church's attitude towards films and the cinema.

[10] S. Bruce, *Religion in the Modern World*.

   This is a distinctly Western perspective, often accompanied by the implication that those who resist the thesis have failed to recognise that being beyond religion is to be culturally advanced, like a snake that has shed its skin. Globally speaking, religion flourishes in many forms, not all of which seem life-enhancing. Even in the West, the secularisation thesis seems less accurate when you bear in mind the burgeoning of interest in 'spirituality', which rides on the back of the apparent failure of religion (and of Christianity in particular). And it is here that the question of what film is doing to people finds a place.

   Religion is unpopular, but a spirituality is something that people seem to 'have' or need by virtue of being human.[11] Either they therefore explicitly tap available mainstream or alternative religious resources (hence, so-called 'pick 'n' mix spirituality'), or they can point to a whole range of activities which have taken the place of organised religion in their lives, whether or not they were ever religious in any formal sense. Three examples of the latter will suffice. Deep allegiance to a football/cricket/rugby/baseball/ice-hockey team becomes almost a reason to live, and shapes a 'liturgical' year.[12] A soap opera provides a central narrative through which a person lives their life. Discussion of the narrative and the issues it raises provides a context for ethical reflection. Identification with and differentiation from leading characters contributes to their own character development. Reflection on episode after episode creates a 'reading community' around which life is structured. For some TV-watchers, reflection on a soap opera may be the only way in which reflection on living happens. A third example is education. 'Lifelong learning' is currently being promoted for many reasons and in many different ways. At its best, it enables people who may not have had or taken earlier opportunities for formal learning to gain confidence in learning, whether for employment purposes, or personal development. When education functions as the primary way in which people discover more about themselves, and develop their sense of self-worth, skills, and self-confidence, it plays a similar role to religion. If one of the possible meanings of 'spirituality' is 'life structure' then lifelong learning can certainly become a life structure which shapes a person's whole approach to living.

   And what of film? I am not suggesting that film-watching has any *unique* claim to have replaced religion in Western culture. Sport, TV and education are but three other contenders.[13] It is,

---

[11] C. Marsh, *Christianity in a Post-Atheist Age*, 23–4, 29–30.
[12] N. Hornby, *Fever Pitch*.
[13] And to these should be added the arts, but possibly also gardening, home design and food/cooking.

however, important to identify ways in which any of these pastimes may be doing more than merely bringing people together for a common purpose, or keeping people entertained. I am thus using film as a case study, both because I am a participant (I am a cinema-goer and film-watcher and also know something about religion 'from the inside'), and because film-watching more than some other similar activities helps me 'get at' the issues in which I am especially interested. To put it bluntly: I could have used sport as my case study, but some of the parallels with religion seem more stretched than with film. Film also seems to provide, as ensuing chapters will make clear, so much more compelling and wide-ranging evidence of having a religion-like function.

Cinema-Going as Religion, or as Substitute for Religion (and is there any difference?)

I am suggesting that cinema-going functions as an alternative to, or a replacement for, traditional religious activity. My concern, though, is to examine the way in which it does not simply fill in the time left by the absence of religion, but actually enables film-watchers to participate in the business of religion. This is the line of thought adopted by John Lyden in his recent *Film as Religion*.[14] I shall begin this section by examining Lyden's approach before going on to clarify, through dialogue with a recent autobio-graphical work by the British journalist John Walsh, the definition of religion with which I am working. What, in short, is the point of considering film-watching and cinema-going as religious activities?

John Lyden's case rests on two basic convictions. First, he con-tends that 'there is no absolute distinction between religion and other aspects of culture'. We have a tendency, he notes, 'to label certain sorts of activities as "religious" chiefly because they fall into patterns that we recognise from religions with which we are famil-iar.'[15] To have a chance of respecting film as a religious/theological resource we need a looser definition of religion, and a more flexible way of understanding how culture and cultures work. Lyden's second conviction is that interpreters of film, theology and culture must respect what films are actually doing in Western society today. Influenced by film critics such as Martin Barker, Lyden is keen to develop an approach which will make sense of films as watched by average film-goers. Though interpretative skill and refined

---

[14] J. Lyden, *Film as Religion: Myths, Morals and Rituals.*
[15] Lyden, *Film as Religion*, 2

analytical methods may be used in examining a film's content, Lyden's view is that no particular skills should be needed to recognise real or hidden filmic meanings. The fact is, Lyden suggests, that films are already functioning religiously, i.e. are offering inspiring and thought-provoking images and worldviews, in relation to which film-goers are exploring and constructing their approaches to living. It is because of this that Lyden develops the religion-film dialogue as an 'inter-religious dialogue', an approach I shall come back to in chapter 6. Lyden has thus latched onto a basic feature of contemporary Western culture. Without devaluing religion, or buying into the secularisation thesis, he is both respecting the *de facto* function of film, and calling for a re-examination of what being religious means. It is intriguing that his approach finds echoes amongst some in the world of film studies.[16]

So far so good. But Lyden is an ally for me as I seek to develop my own position. Though critical of some approaches to the theology/ religion-film dialogue, Lyden remains sympathetic to religious and theological interests. If he notes that some re-thinking is needed on the religion/theology-film scene, he is not claiming that the cinema is replacing religion. He wants to treat film 'as religion' simply in order to get it taken seriously in the world of religious and theological studies within which he moves.

With John Walsh, a British journalist, things are rather different. In *Are You Talking To Me: A Life Through the Movies* (2003), Walsh does not theorise very much about the relationship between religion and the cinema. His humorous and stimulating autobiographical account of his early life is offered as a simple demonstration of the fact that films now provide the narratives through which people discover themselves and make choices about how to live. Religion for Walsh means the Roman Catholic Church, and his life-story supplies evidence of the church's loss of grip upon him, as films helped him make more sense of the life he was living.

The power of cinema for Walsh is clear:

> I grew up mesmerised by the movies. My relationship with the Big Screen was more heady, more intense, more hungrily passionate than my civilised involvement with books, my light flirtations with theatre, my patronising kiss on the forehead of television. Watching films in the dark never seemed to me a passive activity. It was more like visiting a shrine, going to a great dark church for prolonged communion and prayer, even if the only prayers were that Clint Eastwood should waste the bad guys in *A Fistful of Dollars*, or that Julie Christie should find

---

[16] E.g. M. Barker, *From Antz to Titanic: Reinventing Film Analysis*; M. Kermode, *The Shawshank Redemption*.

true love with Alan Bates in *Far From the Madding Crowd*, or that Kim Novak should, at some point, take her clothes off in *Vertigo*.[17]

Walsh's book stands as evidence, then, of how deeply cinema can shape people. The eight films he examines in some detail are related to particular points in his life. But their impact upon his self-discovery is deeper than mere recollection that they 'meant something to him at the time'.[18] Walsh shows how he keeps recalling and reinterpreting scenes from these influential films throughout his life. It is through constant reference to some of these films that he goes on learning and making connections. He suggests that it is the films watched in early life which are especially significant (his auto-biography only takes us through to his early twenties). This may, admittedly, be no different from music and novels, and it is not altogether clear that films retain their power to be influential in later life. It is, however, striking that Walsh was aware, at the age of twenty, that he was 'giving up the Catholic religion and having nothing to put in its place'.[19] He refers to the gap being filled by 'a new, secular obsession about the interconnectedness of things'. This came from his viewing of Nicolas Roeg's *Don't Look Now*. It is also clear that it was the power of the cinema-going experiences throughout his youth and the emotional impact of films upon him which would make the cinema the likely replacement for church.[20]

Lyden and Walsh represent, then, two contemporary interpreters of the film-watching experience who share the sense of the extent of the cultural significance of film. Both want to respect fully what films actually do to people. But different conclusions are being drawn. For Walsh, cinema (perhaps amongst other things) has replaced religion. Or, if religion continues, then it is misguided. For Lyden, films are functioning religiously, but we need to expand our grasp of what 'religion' is to make sense of this cultural development. Lyden may want to take Walsh to task for having such a restricted view of religion. Walsh might simply declare a lack of faith, and suggest – as do many critics of the theology/religion-film debate – that despite his sophistication Lyden is basically wanting

---

[17] J. Walsh, *Are You Talking To Me?: A Life Through the Movies*, 8–9.
[18] The eight films Walsh examine are *Mutiny on the Bounty* (1962), *The Innocents* (1961), *Red River* (1947), *The Sound of Music* (1965), *Bonnie and Clyde* (1967), *Cabaret* (1972), *The Enigma of Kaspar Hauser* (1974) and *'Don't Look Now'* (1973).
[19] Walsh, *Are You Talking To Me?*, 309.
[20] Walsh, *Are You Talking To Me?*, 12–13, 16–17. Deacy notes that the film critic David Thomson records a similar experience, C. Deacy, *Screen Christologies: Redemption and the Medium of Film*, 23.

to rescue religion via his expanded definition. It would clearly be unhelpful to pretend that cultural resources are more explicitly religious than they are. This is not, however, what Lyden is up to. He is not claiming that film is religion in order to rescue religion. He is using religion as a means of clarifying what films are actually doing. Walsh's account of the *de facto* function of film, however, challenges those who want to speak of a film-religion dialogue *at all* to explain why such a dialogue is necessary and useful. If, as Walsh is suggesting, the cinema has replaced the church anyway, then what is the point? There is no dialogue worth having.The value of asking whether cinema-going should be viewed a religious activity is, I suggest, twofold. First, it invites a filmgoer to reflect on the part that films may play in the process of developing a worldview and an ethic. 'Much of the time, we don't even realise the effect that films have on us'.[21] But the complex way in which they move us, get us thinking, compel us to make links and draw contrasts with life-experience past and present indicates that films are doing something important to their viewers. Second, to fail to view film-watching as a religious habit would require scrutiny as to how and where, then, viewers are doing their basic meaning-making. Even if the answer to the question of whether film-watching is religious practice is negative ('it is not in the cinema where I work out the values I live by'), posing the question nevertheless has a useful cultural function.

Through the rest of this book I shall, of course, dispute the view that film-watching has no religious function. Cinema-going and film-watching cannot, in my view, ultimately prove to be wholly satisfactory substitutes for religion. But they are undoubtedly functioning as alternatives to religion in Western cultures today. Both for those who are identifiably religious, and those who are not, they are fulfilling at the very least a religion-like function. But what understanding of 'religion' am I working with to be able to say this?

I am operating with quite a traditional definition, such as that supplied by John Hick: 'an understanding of the universe, together with an appropriate way of living in it, which involves reference beyond the natural world to God, or gods, or to a transcendental order or process'.[22] I shall, though, inevitably be working mostly with an understanding of how religion *functions* in drawing the critical comparison between cinema-going and religious practice. Around the four religion-like aspects of the cinema-going ritual noted at the beginning of this chapter – a regular life-pattern, a

---

[21] Walsh, *Are You Talking To Me?*, 12.
[22] Cited in J. Thrower, *Religion: The Classical Theories*, 5.

respect for rest, participation in shared experience and recognition of a 'holy place' – I am recognising the importance of a cognitive framework which acknowledges respect for a transcendent reality. Am I, then, trying to claim that all film-goers are implicit theists? No, that would be absurd. I am, however, asserting at the outset three things with respect to this working definition. First, more people who watch films are theists of a kind than care to admit it. It is simply that they have not done enough thinking about God in relation to a living tradition of God-talk to bring their feelings, beliefs and thought into some sort of coherent shape. By the end of the book I shall have shown that any exploration of the question of transcendental order is a theological enquiry, and that engagement in God-talk cannot but be existentially and socially useful. Second, the *way* that films often work gets people doing something which is identifiably theological. It is, in other words, not possible to be moved to the core of one's being, or to ask questions about ultimate meaning and value without raising theological questions. Third, the fact that such a process of thinking and believing is evoked by the practices of cinema-going and film-watching is culturally significant. If the churches are not getting theology discussed in the public arena, then this is a cause of sadness. The theology/religion-film dialogue is, however, not a strategy for getting theology discussed publicly via the backdoor. It is a response to the fact that this is where theological discussion – sometimes explicit, sometimes inchoate – is happening already. This book is thus part of the attempt to highlight what is actually going on, and why the religious and theological interpretations of the practices of cinema-going and film-watching are important not just for the identifiably religious.

And What Will Happen to Religion?

If cinema-going and film watching are to be viewed in any sense as religious practices, where does this leave religion as more traditionally understood? This question can only be addressed directly at the end of the enquiry. In this opening chapter I must, however, supply a basic framework within which I approach the question. I can do this with reference to two concepts to which I shall return in Chapter 6: tradition and spirituality. My suggestion that film-watching and cinema-going will not ultimately prove to be satisfactory substitutes for religion cannot alter the fact that religion has to re-find itself in the West.

Walsh's 'autobiography through film' is an intriguing example of how he has used films to locate a set of narratives within which to live, and to understand life. There are other examples in our supposedly secular age of this same need to 'find a tradition'. The popularity of *The Lord of the Rings* both as a book and as a series of films is surely due to the fact that it supplies a whole mythology in relation to which readers and viewers can undertake some fundamental reflection on human living. Whether or not it is indeed to be read as a re-presentation of Christianity is not at issue here. It functions as a tradition-supplying resource. Cinema is thus one of the contemporary channels which supplies narratives for people to 'live within'. By enabling film-goers both to find a tradition and to develop the habit of constantly interacting with the narratives they live within, the habit of cinema-going sharpens a contemporary question: whether *religions* actually achieve in the present what they claim.[23] Perhaps religions have largely stopped achieving what they have in the past. If cinemas fulfil 'religious' functions so strongly today, have religions lost their way? Or is the claim that cinemas have largely taken the place of churches, synagogues, temples and mosques in the West proof that metaphysics is dead, and that most people in the West are simply keeping themselves entertained in preparation for forthcoming oblivion? If religions claim to have better stories, more fulfilling practices, and more truth, then where is the evidence?

A second challenge issued by the religious functioning of film concerns spirituality. The term 'spirituality' is widely used in the contemporary West ('I have a spirituality but I am not religious'). It is being used in at least three senses: to denote a religious faith; to refer more generally to the inner life; to signify a way in which people structure their lives. In referring to the term I must simply acknowledge the ambiguity at this point. Whether or not people consider themselves religious, they still have the task of structuring their lives, and adopting and rejecting particular moral values and philosophical outlooks. They must still decide whether there is an 'inner life' or not. The vast growth of the yoga 'industry' in the West, the expansion of the 'Mind, Body, Spirit' sections in chain bookstores and the evident 'devotion' to fitness regimes which large numbers of people now follow confirm that it is in the midst of these explorations where contemporary religiosity has been relocated for many. Reservations about organised religion are not reflected in a neglect of spirituality in this life-enhancing, life-structuring, health-seeking sense. It will, then, be at least in this realm of contemporary experience that the important cultural/religious function of film and the cinema will need to be explored: where spirituality persists, even whilst religions apparently wane.

---

[23] G. Turner, *Film as Social Practice*, on film and narrative

Of course, the persistence of spirituality does not necessarily prove that people are theists. There are many reasons for organised religion's decline in the West. To point to the fact that religiosity gets diverted does not, though, mean that theism remains intact in a different form. People may have stopped believing in God.[24] The novelist Nick Hornby is an example of a writer who is prepared to admit a keen interest in spirituality, whilst believing that Christianity has had its day. Religions have had a monopoly in the past, and their role has to be re-thought today, especially since, for so many, there is 'nothing out there'.[25] Again, though, things may not prove so simple. To locate the expanding interest in and function of film in Western society – in the context of resistance to religion but support for spirituality – requires us to re-examine many features of both cinema-going and religion. Because films do things to people on many levels (psychological, social, spiritual, moral, philosophical), they need closer scrutiny.

The focus of this study is therefore on what films actually do to people and on what people do with their film-watching. I approach the task as someone interested in religion, hence the content of this first chapter. The two worlds of film and religious studies inhabit the same space, however, when it comes to the evident cultural function of film. What follows, therefore, can be considered a contribution to cultural studies. If it may appear to some to have an apologetic purpose, then this is only because of the blind spot which becomes evident in interdisciplinary studies when it comes to religion. It is not the main aim of this study to deal with that blind spot, though this may come about as a by-product. My main purpose is to ask how theology is to be done, given that film – as an example of an increasingly significant cultural medium – is getting the supposedly 'non-religious' to do a theology-like thing anyway.

---

[24] S. Bruce, 'The Problems of a Liberal Religion: A Sociologist's View', in M.D. Chapman (ed.), *The Future of Liberal Theology*, 221–41.
[25] N. Hornby, *How to Be Good*; 244; C. Marsh, 'Sex, Shopping, and Other Weighty Theological Matters (1)', *Epworth Review* 31/1 (Jan. 2004), 27.

Case-Study A

Cinema-Going in 2001

What impact might a regular habit of cinema-going have upon a person? Even allowing for the fact that it obviously depends on the viewer, and the location of the habit within their overall life-structure, there are nevertheless conclusions that can be drawn from the films on offer. Scrutiny of UK releases throughout 2001 leads to some telling insights.

Had a person gone weekly to the cinema for the first quarter of 2001, watching the films that were most heavily publicised and thus likely to prove 'blockbusters', they would have seen five of the films that eventually featured in the twenty most-watched films of the year: *Cast Away*, *What Women Want*, *Hannibal*, *The Emperor's New Groove* and *Miss Congeniality*.[1] Of these, only one, *Cast Away*, could be considered to have received anything approaching 'critical acclaim'. Tom Hanks' Oscar-nominated performance led to the suggestion that the film is 'metaphysics for the masses' (*Independent* 13.1.01). That apart, Mel Gibson (*What Women Want*), Disney (*The Emperor's New Groove*), Sandra Bullock and others (*Miss Congeniality*) and Anthony Hopkins as Hannibal Lecter (*Hannibal*) are likely to have been the reasons behind their box-office success. As far as the consequences of viewing are concerned, a Disney film and two romantic comedies may not have lingered in the mind, whilst *Hannibal* might have left some disturbing scenes in the memory.

By contrast, had our imaginary cinema-goer viewed all films rated as four or five stars in the *Independent* during the same period, then in addition to *Cast Away* they would have watched: *Crouching Tiger, Hidden Dragon*, *Requiem for a Dream*, *Sexy Beast*, *Traffic*, *The Low Down*, *Songs from the Second Floor*, *Shadow of the Vampire*, *Best in Show*, *Dark Days*, *Audition*,

---

[1] Their top twenty positions being thirteenth, eleventh, sixth, twentieth and eighteenth, respectively. For such listings, see the British Film Institute's website < www.bfi.org.uk >.

Brother, and *Save the Last Dance*. Comparing this alternative list of films with the critical judgments of published movie guides[2] would leave five films worth watching: *Crouching Tiger, Hidden Dragon*, *Requiem for a Dream*, *Traffic*, *Songs from the Second Floor* and *Best in Show*.[3] Two of these were shown in multiplexes (*Crouching Tiger, Hidden Dragon* and *Traffic*), the other three in independent film theatres.

Sampling later in the same year (October and November) reveals a similar pattern. Three of the films released during that two-month period featured in the year's top twenty: *American Pie 2*, *The Others* and *Harry Potter and the Philosopher's Stone*.[4] This time, two of the films were judged successful artistically (*The Others* and *Harry Potter and the Philosopher's Stone*). In addition to these two, according to the *Independent*'s film critics, a cinema-goer would, however, have benefited from also seeing: *Amélie*, *A Bench in the Park*, *La Ville est Tranquille*, *Princess Mononoke*, *The Man Who Wasn't There*, *Eureka*, *The Piano Teacher*, *Ghost World*, *Disco Pigs*, *Kandahar* and *In Praise of Love*. Again cross-referencing with other assessments, this list can in turn be reduced to *Amélie*, *The Man Who Wasn't There*, *Ghost World*, and *Kandahar*.[5]

This simple exercise occasions perhaps no great surprise. The films that do best at the box office are rarely the critics' favourites. The films which critics prefer are rarely shown at multiplexes anyway (and so are not likely to become blockbusters). Of the films that most people go to see, there are not a great many that appear to set out to linger in the mind, or to carry an emotional impact beyond the actual viewing. Film-watching may thus, after all, prove to be wholly to do with time-limited entertainment: forgotten almost as soon as the first slice of pizza is picked up at the post-film meal.

All forms of film criticism and interaction with film that focus upon what viewers do with film, however, will not be content with such a simple conclusion. For one thing, the division between multiplexes and independent film theatres, and the emphasis upon the top twenty box-office successes, hide the many relatively successful films which show at both types of venue. For another, the impact of films cannot always easily be predicted. *The Shawshank*

---

[2] K. Fane-Saunders, *Radio Times Guide to Films*; J. Walker (ed.) *Halliwell's Film and Video Guide 2004*.

[3] i.e. Films rated with at least four stars in Fane-Saunders 2001 and with at least two stars in Walker 2003a.

[4] Ninth, sixteenth and first, respectively.

[5] Using films rated two or more stars in Walker (ed.), *Halliwell's* (*A Bench in the Park* and *Princess Mononoke* not being listed).

Redemption was a slow-starter at the box office, which picked up in popularity and significance when it appeared on video. Without being an art-house movie buff, a weekly cinema-goer in 2001 in the UK may also have viewed *Unbreakable, Quills,* and *Chocolat* in the first quarter. During October and November he or she could also have watched *The Pledge, Legally Blonde* and *Down from the Mountain.* There are, in other words, films around which do not merely seek blockbuster success, which resist art-house categorisation, and yet which may stimulate and provoke their viewers to feel and to think in ways which transcend the charge of their being 'mere entertainment', even whilst they entertain. It is precisely along this path – moving in both directions: towards blockbusters and art-house films – that the religious critic and theologian, in the company of those film-critics who want to take audience responses seriously, will want to tread.

In the context of a film-watching habit, the randomness of the subject matter dealt with in film and the range of moods and emotions evoked by films is striking. Granted that a cinema-going habit which shifted location (from multiplex to theatre) would offer a still wider range of viewing experiences, even regular attendance at the same multiplex would offer a diversity of stimuli: cognitive, ethical, aesthetic and affective.

A critical question for this present enquiry is how such a habit is like and unlike weekly attendance at a church. The latter offers a regular diet (scripture reading – sometimes within a set annual pattern [lectionary], interpretation of text or theme [sermon/address], set framework [liturgy]) in a set location (same time, same place). The same (biblical/theological) themes thus recur throughout the church-going experience, though might be presented in diverse forms of literature (within the Bible, for example, as historical or history-like narrative, as poetry, or as letters).

Two major differences are evident even at the level of sociological comparison between church- and cinema-going. Churchgoing is usually attached to some sense of 'belonging' to a community. Infrequent attenders may still retain some sense of belonging to a particular congregation, even if they do not choose to call themselves 'committed'. By contrast, even regular cinema-goers are unlikely to feel any sense of 'belonging' to a multiplex chain, even those who hold an annual membership. The transaction is, after all, commercial. The one exception may be members of independent film theatres keen to see smaller theatres flourish, in relation to which some sense of a 'cinema-going community' may emerge, and amongst whom a sense of public, educational responsibility may also thrive.

Second, church-going happens within some sense of an assumed unity lying behind (often very diverse) Christian practices. Though a single theological framework – 'orthodoxy' – is notoriously difficult to pinpoint behind Christian practice, church-going nevertheless relates to something which must be identifiably 'Christian', lest Christianity lose all sense of identity. By contrast, film-watching relates to no single ideological framework. Cinema-going entails exposure to a wide range of ideological frameworks. Of course, film criticism itself entails critical scrutiny of such a view. Films shown, at multiplexes especially, may not draw on as broad a range of ideological frameworks as may at first be supposed. Hollywood has a limited outlook. But Hollywood is not everything; nor is Hollywood univocal. Furthermore, even Hollywood cannot wholly control what films actually do. Cinemas therefore create a different kind of space from churches for audiences/congregations to undergo experiences, reflect on what is happening to them, develop their identities, and to decide how to live. But there are some similar things going on.

2

Audiences, Congregations, Entertainment, Worship

This chapter is about groups of people and the purposes for, and contexts in, which they meet. It is about audiences and congregations. A study of contemporary cinema-going as in any sense a 'religious' practice must inevitably address the question of how cinema-going may or may not relate to worship. If worship is the focal point of religious practice, then do cinema-going and film-watching supplement participation in worship, run parallel to it, function *as* worship and thus replace worship as we know it, or do something else?[1]

Worship as Entertainment[2]

Not so long ago I commented in a lecture that large preaching centres in British cities in the late 1950s functioned, in effect, as Sunday evening entertainment for many of those present. These were places to meet friends, to hear good rhetoric, to be moved and stimulated, to catch up on local and world news. That such things happened in the context of rousing hymn-singing, public praying

---

[1] I am aware that the assumption that worship is central to religious practice could itself be challenged e.g. by the view that the 'point' of religion is to enable people to live a God-/religion-inspired life. This is not a point I can take up here. I merely wish to address the question of what is actually happening in film-watching and how this relates to what is commonly known as worship. For an expression of the centrality of worship in the Christian life, consider Gray's statement: 'For Christians worship is the pivotal activity that focuses and enriches life, giving meaning and purpose to existence'. See D. Gray, 'Worship' in A. Hastings, A. Mason and H. Pyper (eds.), *The Oxford Companion to Christian Thought*, 762.
[2] A version of the opening paragraphs of this section are due to appear in C. Marsh, 'Sex, Shopping, and Other Weighty Theological Matters (2)', *Epworth Review* 31/2 (April 2004).

and overt Christian interpretation of all that was presented would have been fundamental for many, an added bonus for some, and endured under sufferance by others. These major, weekly, rhetorical 'events' had, I suggested, been replaced for most people by a wide range of alternatives, not least Friday evening TV 'review-of-the-week' shows, meals out with friends and family, and Sunday newspapers. In the process, Christian interpretation of, and reflection on, major issues had largely disappeared from the public domain. Furthermore, within the private world of Christianity (given how enclosed many churches often became), it would no longer be in churches that people would primarily expect to receive insight and comment on news, or to be stimulated by rhetoric. News and comment would be differently received, and entertainment would be enjoyed through a wide range of newer media.

I received two main responses to the suggestion. The first, in the public discussion of my lecture immediately afterwards, was critical. My questioner argued that I was underplaying the profound spiritual importance of those occasions for the majority of those present. The reason that people in the 1940s and 1950s queued to hear the 'great preachers' was that they would expect to be uplifted spiritually. Regular attendance was spiritual formation. The second response, uttered to me quietly in private after the session, seemed much more positive. I was exactly right, said my respondent. There was a direct correlation between what occurred on a Saturday evening in such preaching centres (social events) and what happened on a Sunday (a service of worship): it was all of a piece. People came because they were part of the whole scene.

Both responses can, of course, be seen as legitimate and accurate. There is no doubt that I overplayed my point to make my case. I do not doubt the very real spiritual formation which occurred for many through such sermon-focused services of worship. But I am also realistic enough (and pleased!) to know that what my second respondent indicated was grist to my mill. In the context of 1950s Britain, when churches often functioned for people as 'total institutions', offering to meet all spiritual and social needs, the assumption that basic, informed, theological and spiritual formation was consciously happening for all is misplaced. Whatever the intent of those leading it, or those interpreting it with hindsight, worship was often being received, and thus functioning, in a very similar fashion to entertainment.

Evidence that this must have been so is supplied by what soon happened with the advent of television. Two events have been noted to have had a decisive impact on the British scene. The first was the launch of Independent Television (ITV) in 1955. The airing of

Sunday Night at the London Palladium proved a major challenge for Sunday evening congregations. Congregations declined.[3] The second was the airing on BBC television of *The Forsyte Saga* in 1967. Many who had remained loyal to Sunday evening worship throughout the early 1960s found they could do so no longer when faced with a major dramatisation of a literary classic. Congregations declined again.[4]

Such developments interweave with the general pattern of increasing secularisation in British society throughout the 1960s, the full picture of which I cannot explore here.[5] For our immediate purposes I simply make four observations. First, the switch from Sunday worship to television or other activities may indicate a loss of religious conviction. Alternatively, second, the decline of attendance at Christian worship may demonstrate the limited nature of the supposed conviction and/or the fact that the religious practice engaged in was being 'accessed' for other than religious reasons. The new practice may, in other words, have more continuity with the old than may be supposed, although neither religious conviction nor the desire to worship were the primary ground of that continuity. Although this is scarcely welcome news with regard to the nature and extent of religious observance in Britain prior to the 1960s, it may nevertheless prove highly instructive.

---

[3] For statistics on church attendance and affiliation, see e.g. C. Brown, *The Death of Christian Britain*, chs.7–8.

[4] '*The Forsyte Saga* was the BBC's last major drama to be produced in black and white ... It was the serial which put BBC 2 on the map, attracting six million viewers on Sunday evenings, disrupting church services and emptying pubs' (J. Evans, *The Penguin TV Companion*, 266). Juxtaposing this observation with the point about *Sunday Night at the London Palladium* leads to an intriguing (perhaps class-related) speculation. If ITV's appearance had relatively little direct effect on church attendance, because TV-watchers were not by and large church-goers, then BBC 2's appearance may have had a greater impact. That the arrival of commercial television had a profound impact on British cinemas is noted in Jancovich and Faire, *Audience*, 139–40: '... unlike the BBC, it did not have the educational, highbrow image which alienated so many of the cinema audience'.

[5] For more, see e.g. G. Davie, *Religion in Britain Since 1945: Believing Without Belonging* and *Religion in Modern Europe*; S. Bruce, *Religion in Modern Britain* and *Religion in the Modern World*; Brown, *Death of Christian Britain* and Marsh, *Christianity in a Post-Atheist Age*. Marwick's concern in his comprehensive, and juicily opinionated, study of the 1960s is not primarily to chart and comment on religious developments. But his work is invaluable here nevertheless. See A. Marwick, *The Sixties: Cultural Revolution in Britain, France, Italy, and the United States, c.1958–c.1974*.

An uncomfortable truth may be, third, that the nature or lack of continuity between Christianity before and after the mass availability of TV contributed to the increase in secularisation throughout the 1960s and 1970s.[6] In other words, Christianity in Britain after *Sunday Night at the London Palladium* and *The Forsyte Saga* simply was not interesting enough. For 'interesting' we may in part read 'entertaining'. I do not, however, want to suggest that all-singing, all-dancing worship would have remedied a situation of decline then, any more than it is likely to do now. I simply offer this third point as a contribution towards understanding how Christianity developed in Britain through the 1960s and 1970s. Either it turned inwards and suggested to its participants that they look to their inner lives, supported through this trying, secular time by churches/groups which became increasingly detached from wider society as time progressed.[7] Or, individual Christians turned radically outwards causing many to turn their attentions beyond Christianity altogether, even while serving important social and political causes, leaving them unclear as to how socially and politically committed the churches really would prove to be.[8]

Fourth, it is highly likely that many people became Sunday evening television-viewers whilst heaving a huge sigh of relief. A pattern of churchgoing (twice on Sunday) was broken. A pattern of social behaving was broken. For many this would have been liberating. The difficulty is that in many parts of British Christianity, the assumptions about the 'basic pattern of churchgoing' remained, and in some quarters remain even now. British Christianity still wrestles, in other words, with a pattern of Christian behaviour forged in a pre-technological age. In some cases, indeed, as I can see from my own tradition (Methodism), this pattern remains, and those who assume it and practise it are the ones who chose for

---

[6] Though this obviously needs further empirical investigation.

[7] This tendency is not to be equated with any single denomination or grouping. Many evangelicals would, of course, have taken up this stance, though only until 1974 when, as a result of the Lausanne Covenant, many in the evangelical tradition re-found their social conscience. On all of this see e.g. A. Hastings, *A History of English Christianity 1920–1985*, Parts VI and VII, here esp. 615–17.

[8] This is often the reading given by those who consider that the decline of Christianity in Britain is 'the fault of the liberals', for having been too accommodationist throughout this period. At this point, I think, the history really does need to be rewritten, not to deny what happened, but to evaluate differently what can be known. There are huge theological, ecclesiastical and socio-cultural implications and consequences following on from how this period is evaluated.

whatever reason not to break free from it.[9] Churchgoing of the 'twice on a Sunday' form is thus a conservative ('traditional') social practice in the sense that it cannot accommodate *The Forsyte Saga*-watchers and their contemporary equivalents. As a practice, it has failed to accommodate those who wanted to be 'entertained' else-where. Furthermore, though worship is clearly a social practice which demands a time commitment, the question of how and whether worship and entertainment inter-relate in any significant way has rarely been posed in this context.

These four observations challenge contemporary understand-ings of worship. They may lead us to conclude that we must lure people to worship through offering more entertaining features – for example, the worship leader as game-show host, or more quizzes. I *do* think that worship could be made more 'entertaining'. But I want to use the historical and contemporary evidence very carefully indeed and offer such an assertion with great caution as I suggest in what sense the 'entertainment' emphasis is legitimate with respect to worship and in what sense not.[10]

What types of worship flourish? Sifting through the evidence across a wide range of traditions, three features seem prominent. First, worship needs to be *participative*. 'Participation' can be understood in a number of ways. It can mean lively singing, liturgi-cal responses, structured conversation, public praying. Of course, attention to, and personal use of, whatever a leader introduces into worship should be a means of participation. Greek or Russian Orthodox worship can be considered, against this background, as participative as the most raucous charismatic 'praise event'. But we

---

[9] I do, though, need to note one important qualification (which itself signals a need for further study). In some contexts the pattern of churchgo-ing was not twice on Sunday; Sunday evening was the main service due to Saturday morning working, i.e. Sunday morning provided the only oppor-tunity for a 'lie-in'. For some, the breaking of that pattern by a change in Sunday evening habits might have signalled a more significant drifting away from the church altogether. Commitment to churchgoing might only have been more easily sustainable for those for whom the switch to the centrality of Sunday morning worship (as indeed happened in British Methodism throughout the 1960s and 1970s) was a viable option. I am grateful to Brian Beck for discussion on this point.

[10] Full development of this point clearly lies beyond the scope of this book, which is merely exploring how film, as an example of a quite complex form of 'entertainment', actually functions. By worship being more 'enter-taining' in addition to the points to follow in the main text I mean, for example, being scrupulously well-prepared, sensitive to space and time, and focused on the experience of all those present.

need to accept that some forms of worship are more obviously participative than others, more reflective forms being favoured by particular personality types.

Second, worship needs to be *moving*. The success of many of the preaching centres of the past was surely due to the influence of the rhetorical flourishes of preachers upon people as much as the content of sermons. People recall things because of being moved by the oratory. Similarly in the present, it is often emphasised that worship is much more than preaching. Hymns and other music, colour, visual imagery, silence, the smell of incense, the rhythm and poetry of liturgical prayer all contribute to worship as a moving, multi-sensory experience. In such a context, too – and especially for church traditions which place great emphasis upon preaching – a dull, unmoving sermon becomes all the more apparent.

Third, worship needs to be *connected* to the rest of life. I choose the word 'connected' rather than 'relevant' in order to indicate a relationship to daily living, without implying that the link is always simple and straightforward. Liturgical worship, for example, in making use of ancient traditions, may need 'living within' on a regular basis in order for its connectedness with the rest of life to be apparent. Liturgy shapes life, as well as being influenced by life.[11] Its words and images become increasingly meaningful and helpful not merely in the context of the services in which they are first, or regularly, uttered but throughout daily living. Many of the dimensions of participation in Holy Communion may not be instantly apparent to a new believer. The full import of Communion as a 'messianic banquet' to which all are invited, where all are fed, and its function therefore as stimulus to the purchase of fair trade produce, for example, may need some teasing out. But *disconnected* worship can occur. Even if there is an element of 'taking time out' in worship, to participate in a routine which is different from the other routines of life, connected worship is not escapism. It is worship that is disconnected, and thus escapist, which is irrelevant.

It will be noted that I have not chosen to include in the above three features references such as 'God-centred', Christ-centred' or 'Spirit-filled'. This is simply because I am prepared to accept that any kind of worship can be all three of these. Limited though my enquiry is at this point, I am, of course, focusing upon aspects of worship as pertaining to the worshipper's experience rather than the theological considerations lying behind how and why worship might be termed 'effective'.[12] These three features of contemporary

---

[11] Though in the latter case, the process is often quite slow.
[12] I should also add that I do not exclude the possibility that any cinema-visit could in principle be God-centred, Christ-centred or Spirit-filled.

worship are nevertheless striking. It is not in any simple sense worship's overtly contemporary character, its liveliness or its immediate relevance which make it attractive. Nor is it pandering to consumer demand to point out that worship can 'do' something to and for a person. This has always been so.[13] Where people have wanted to worship, there has always been an acknowledgement that it has value.[14] If these features do not constitute 'entertainment' it would nevertheless be quite wrong to underplay the fact that they are continuous with the types of human experience which have proved to offer alternatives to worship as it has often been known in the recent past. And it is precisely such features as these – participation, the affective, connectedness with living[15] – which remind us of how and why cinema-going and film-watching must be brought closely alongside the practice of worship in the present.[16] But where will this close association lead?

Film Within Worship

One initial step which may be taken is to use film within worship as currently known. Within the constraints of copyright law, visual imagery is widely used in forms of so-called 'alternative worship'.[17]

---

[13] Marsh, Christianity in a Post-Atheist Age, 9.

[14] Much is, of course, often made of the fact that in the past, adherence to Christianity has been enforced. Whether people involved themselves willingly or unwillingly in Christian worship is of crucial significance. We may also have to accept that in 1950s Britain (and earlier) some people will have worshipped and been connected to churches because there was not much else to do. It must further be acknowledged that it is easy to claim too much for worship as a practice if it assumed that it will always have a profound impact on its participants. Here is a point at which the critical comparison with cinema-going proves helpful. On the one hand, not all films 'work' for all viewers (as worship cannot 'move' everyone every week). On the other hand, a good film, watched many times, is precisely like the 'non-identical repetition' of good worship. 'The ritual quality in film viewing is generally exposed when audiences see the same film repeatedly ... This aspect of film ... is often argued but it is invoked every time someone says to us in a darkened cinema: "Here it comes, watch this bit!"': Turner, *Film as Social Practice*, 116.

[15] It is striking how these overlap with the interests of Martin Barker. See Barker, *From Antz to Titanic*, 3–5, 13–16, 28-31, 33–7, 47–8, 70, 104, 175, 193–4.

[16] Hughes is frequently critical of the impact of entertainment upon worship. See G. Hughes, *Worship as Meaning: A Liturgical Theology for Late Modernity*, 156, 164, 174–5, 183.

[17] This, of course, invites the question: 'alternative to what?' to which the answer usually has to be, 'dull, boring services'. The notion of 'alternative'

Though this is often a case of Protestants catching up with the use of the visual as long since used in Roman Catholic and Orthodox worship,[18] the use of moving imagery is a contemporary development, made possible by the ready (even if still quite expensive) availability of sophisticated electronic technology.[19] The use of film in such a setting is, in formal terms, no different from using a choir to contribute to worship, or asking someone to sing a solo or to offer a reading (whether scriptural or not) 'with feeling'.

But what would a use of film within worship amount to? I offer three examples. The first and most obvious use is *film as text*. A film-clip is here used in the same way as a reading may be used in a sermon. It introduces into worship a resource to be interpreted. It may be chosen to coincide with a scriptural reading, so that a sermon/address then interprets a reading via a film-clip. Two examples of this would be: a showing of part of the final meal from *Babette's Feast* in relation to a meal participated in by Jesus in the Gospels; the clip from *Schindler's List* when Schindler is approached by the Perlmans' daughter urging him to bring about their release from the concentration camp, alongside a reading of Matthew 21.28–32. When used appropriately, films do not simply illustrate 'the' meaning of a biblical text through such juxtaposition. They provide prompts for creative interpretation.[20] The interplay of the three voices – biblical text, filmic text, preacher as interpreter – then invites the hearer (worshipper) into the interpretative act. The presence of three voices itself counters the view that preaching is simply a matter of an authoritative interpreter *telling* the congregation what a text *means*. The use of film thus contributes to the notion of God 'speaking' in between and through the

---

[17] (*continued*) cannot, for example, be used simply to indicate 'non-liturgical' as an alternative to 'liturgical' for many of the alternative forms use liturgy (often pre-modern forms). Nor is hymnody (or participatory singing) wholly neglected, despite the greater emphasis on a wide range of recorded music. For more on this, see e.g. J. Baker and D. Gay, *Alternative Worship*, who, whilst being very helpful re. 'still' visual arts, are strangely silent on film. This could admittedly be due largely to copyright issues (on which see 'Using Film with Integrity' in I. Maher, *Faith and Film: Close Encounters of an Evangelistic Kind*, 27).

[18] And thus getting over their recent, though in part Reformation-inspired, logocentric enslavement to aspects of modernity which, with the exception of Pentecostal/charismatic revivals, overemphasised word (and mind) at the expense of the visual and the affective (and the heart).

[19] I am thinking here of video- and data-projectors, laptop computers and high quality, integrated sound systems.

[20] Baker and Gay, *Alternative Worship*, xv.

multiple voices seeking to interpret the Word of God (in Scripture and world) today.

The second possible use of film in worship is for the purpose of what may be termed *liturgical enhancement*. Under this heading I include the use of film-clips at appropriate points within a structured service which amplify what is going on at that particular time.[21] A good example here is the use of a six- or nine-minute clip from *The Mission* in which Mendoza (De Niro) drags the armour of his former life as a slave-trader up the mountain to the top of the waterfall, only to have the bundle cut from him by one of those whom he had formerly sought to enslave. It is powerful in its own right. When used alongside prayers of confession, the clip becomes yet more powerful, as worshippers are invited by the clip into the full significance of the act in which they are engaged. A public prayer of confession could either precede or follow the showing of the clip. As Bryan Stone has noted:

> The road to forgiveness through penance is one that Protestant churches have generally rejected since the Reformation of the sixteenth century with its attack on a deteriorated system that reduced salvation to a crude, mechanical transaction between the individual and the church. *The Mission*, however, offers a stirring portrayal of the capacity for penance to serve as a meaningful and authentic path to salvation – one that engages the whole person, body and soul, in turning from sin to forgiveness.[22]

In being used in Protestant settings, this clip can highlight the power of forgiveness in a fresh way, which public, oral confession and absolution often do not. Worshippers are invited, without direct recourse to the practice of penance, nevertheless to consider what burdens they 'carry' in a similar way.[23]

Other parts of a service could likewise be liturgically enhanced by film. Prayers of intercession could be prompted by appropriate clips (with or without sound) in the same way that still images are now often used, when people are encouraged to 'pray with their

---

[21] 'Amplify' must be taken here to mean 'extend' or 'develop' and not merely 'illustrate'.

[22] B.P. Stone, *Faith and Film: Theological Themes at the Cinema*, 146.

[23] It must be acknowledged also that the potential emotional power of the clip, for those who have never seen it, can create difficulties e.g. if a person feels 'burdened' in a way for which there is no resolution in the manner provided for Mendoza in the film. This is, however, always a potential aspect of worship. It cannot always be predicted what worship will do to people, and thus what God is doing and can do through it.

eyes open', literally and metaphorically. Prayers of dedication can be enhanced by clips of characters who resolve to make a new start, or amend their lives in some way. The point is not to offer filmic material as commentary upon what is happening at a particular point in a service, but to allow film to facilitate the liturgical activity being engaged in at that point. A question that arises with all such clips, of course, is how often they can be used effectively in this way. Weekly use would be inappropriate. But as with any feature of worship, repetition is not in itself a problem. It is whether overuse leads to ineffective worship.

The third possible use of film in worship is arguably the most controversial: *mood-setting*. It could equally be called 'preparation for worship', although mood-setting is not confined to what happens prior to worship. The mood of worship can be set at various points throughout a service. Again, in formal terms this is no different from what already happens when particular music is selected, or silence is kept, at appropriate points within worship. It is simply the medium through which the mood is set that is different.

Again, clips can be used with or without sound.[24] Moving images of open spaces (deserts, landscapes, space) can create a mood of awe. Such mood-setting need not, however, always be meditative and reflective. In a setting in which children are present, even Disney's *The Jungle Book* ('The King of the Swingers', where Balou 'loses it') can be a form of preparation for worship. It is suggestive in both form and content of the appropriate 'lostness' which can occur in worship.

What criteria should operate in these three uses of film within worship? Obviously, a clip used in worship should be relatively short and self-contained, requiring minimal introduction. Worship is not a training session or a seminar. Time taken to 'talk around' a clip can become like commentating on what is happening: it prevents worship being worship. A clip is there to facilitate worship. If much commentary is needed then it is probably not an appropriate clip, although appropriately contextualising of a clip within a film's narrative will be necessary.

Secondly, a clip should be used in a way that retains the integrity of the whole film. Inappropriate extraction would be misuse. Theological interpretation of seemingly non-theological texts is perfectly legitimate. But what constitutes 'inappropriate extraction' is the

---

[24] To use a film-clip without the sound intended to accompany it does, however, raise the charge that films are here being plundered for an inappropriate use. I shall address this shortly.

crucial question. Sometimes associations are too easily made between Christian belief and scenes in films and the nature of a link between text and interpretation is not well thought through.[25] It is unlikely that on the evening before a service a leader of worship would be able to think of a fresh clip to use. Preparation of a clip usually needs 'mulling time' – time during which its appropriateness to function as text, liturgical enhancement or mood-setting becomes apparent.[26]

There is, admittedly, a very basic charge to be drawn against the use of film-clips at all. The full power of film depends on good quality screen images, high quality sound, a context in which viewers can be attentive and, above all, a setting in which the whole of a film can be watched. Film-clips by definition limit film's power, especially if shown in contexts not conducive to appropriate attentiveness. Rather than accept the charge that clips should not be used at all, however, I offer two counter-arguments. First, in formal terms, the use of a clip is exactly the same as using a lectionary passage from the Bible: a small part is used, though really the hearer needs to go and read the whole thing, know how it all hangs together, what its main points are, and how useful it is to read. The parallel is not perfect, of course. The Bible is more composite and diverse than most films. But the point stands that the Bible cannot be read in its entirety every week.

Second, I want to use the very existence of film-trailers as an argument for the use of clips in worship. In the same way that no use of a lectionary passage of the Bible is meant to stand as a replacement for the impact of the whole collection of writings which make up the Bible, so also the playing of a film-clip is not meant to stand for the whole. It is *intended* that hearers and viewers open themselves up to the whole 'text'. In the case of films, this means that

---

[25] This leads to critiques made of much theology and film discussion by Steve Nolan, who notes the ease with which 'cinematic analogues' of religious themes are located and explored. I shall consider this objection in Chapter 6.

[26] It can, of course, be argued that the contextual use of a clip within worship automatically abuses a film, i.e. text, liturgical enhancement or mood-setting prevent a film's being a film by determining its meaning in the context of worship. This does not follow. To offer a meaning through contextualising any 'text' does not inevitably abuse it; indeed, how could it? Contextualization of a text in worship merely offers an interpretation of a particular clip. It will be one amongst many, and open to challenge as an interpretation. It would only be abuse of a film or clip if it could be shown that its use in worship wholly failed to respect the film as a film.

clips used should imply that it will be profitable for worshippers to view the whole film.[27]

The second criterion does, though, instantly suggest a third: if the whole of a film cannot be recommended for viewing, then a clip should probably not be used at all. Whether this criterion should apply only to worship is a moot point.[28] But considering film-clips as trailers links with the 'connectedness' of worship: worshippers are encouraged to relate their worship with their consumption of art and media. They are thus invited by the clips to watch the film. Having watched a clip in the context of worship, they are in turn invited to relate their response to the film back to worship. In implicitly recommending that a whole film be watched, however, this third criterion reminds leaders of worship of the immense significance of using any form of art within worship.

Film is, however, in this case ceasing to function as 'entertainment'. By relocation within the context of worship, film is certainly being respected as more than 'mere entertainment'. It is art which can find an appropriate place as part of worship (like a poem, an anthem, a sculpture, a flute solo, a painting, a dance or a banner[29]). But the fact that films are often associated with 'mere entertainment' can be a plus point. Their use within worship is a highly contemporary way of indicating how the stuff of life – film-watching as a broader cultural practice – dovetails with the practice of worshipping. The substance of this whole discussion, furthermore, should encourage liturgists to think even more critically about their theory and practice, and students of cultural studies to ask whether a film is ever only a film.

The drawback of the use of film is signalled in my comments both on the first use of film (as text) and on the second and third

---

[27] Unlike the use of lectionary readings this need not, of course, mean that a film's ideological slant or purpose is commended even whilst its viewing is recommended. But too stark a contrast with the Bible should not be drawn here. Use of lectionary passages may mean that the overall message of the Bible is commended, whilst not necessarily all of its component parts. Such an observation merely raises, of course, the question of how the authority of the Bible is to be understood and its diverse texts to be used.

[28] In educational settings, for example, things would be quite different. In church life, however, other factors also come into play. Use of a clip from a film the rating for which exceeds the age of some of those present, for example, is even more of an issue than for trailers shown in cinemas.

[29] Some of these examples of art can, of course, be viewed in their entirety in worship. However, many artistic works that are used are often extracts (an anthem from an oratorio, a movement from a long piece of music). Furthermore, much art used in worship takes the form of reproduction (e.g. of a painting, or a picture of a sculpture).

criteria (retention of integrity, recommending whole films). Film can all too easily be used simply illustratively, like a story in a sermon, so that the 'point' of use swamps the film/story itself. This undervalues film as a medium. The emotional power of film, even through an appropriately chosen film-clip, can do more than illustrate a preacher's message or provide a helpful visual background in a service of worship. By being memorable, it keeps on working in the mind and heart of the viewer. That is how a good film works anyway. It is also how films used in worship can work. Where a film-clip is used for illustrative purposes only, however, then the emotional and aesthetic power of film are being inadequately respected. Furthermore, such an illustrative use of film fails to respect how worship itself actually 'works', especially in a contemporary hermeneutical climate which stresses the role of the receiver (the worshipper and the film-watcher) as much as the 'sign-maker' (film director, worship leader) in an interpretative act. It is true that films can only exert their full impact (emotionally, aesthetically, cognitively and ethically) when watched in their entirety. But clips can and do carry immense power in themselves when appropriately selected.

Entertainment as Worship

There is, however, an even broader and more challenging dimension to the question of the relationship between worship and film. This second area of exploration gets us much closer to the set of questions with which this book is primarily dealing. What of those who are not worshippers in any traditional sense, yet who may be moved and provoked by film, and who may indeed have similar reactions to those who are provoked by the use of film within formal worship? If, as I argued in chapter 1, cinema-going and film-watching do function in a religion-like way, then what forms of worship do they produce?

I cannot enter here into the full complexity of issues surrounding the overlap and distinction between entertainment and worship. It may not prove possible to speak of entertainment per se, or worship per se, and make a comparison. Stand-up comedy, vaudeville, theatre, lap-dancing, opera, mime, magic and many other forms of human activity may count as 'entertainment'. Different forms of entertainment raise different issues as far as their capacity to be contexts in which the worship of God is possible. As far as film is concerned, however, it is important to address film's capacity to entertain so that theology's interaction with *popular* culture is handled, lest this book veer too much towards an esoteric discussion of film as 'high culture'.[30]

We must first review the arguments for and against seeing film-watching as a religious practice in relation to a working definition of worship. Worship can be defined in a variety of ways. In most general terms it is 'a *religious* phenomenon, a reaching out *through* the fear that always accompanies the sacred to the *mysterium* conceived as *tremendum* but also *fascinans*, because behind it and in it there is an intuition of the Transcendent'.[31] The focus of this definition, then, is the awe-inspiring, spine-tingling sense of 'otherness' *felt* by the worshipper. Still in general terms, but related more to practices, worship can be defined as: 'prayer, especially public prayer, the honour expressed through praise, thanksgiving, and acknowledgement given to God by believing communities in word, symbol, and action'.[32] The focus here is on a range of activities which are conceived in terms of what worshippers are doing in response to God's being, presence and activity. A third definition is supplied within a detailed contemporary study of the way that worship and liturgy 'work'. In a stimulating but complex study of 'worship as meaning', Graham Hughes locates the defining characteristic of worship as bringing people 'to the frontier', to the edge of what is known. Worship that has meaning becomes an enacted practice, a space within which 'border crossings' are negotiated: by representative people (worship leaders) or by all worshipping participants. Worship is a context in which the interplay of transcendence and immanence, the beyond and the here and now, is explored in such a way that it has an impact on the whole of life.[33]

All the above-cited definitions were worked out by (male) Christian writers who indicate awareness of the wider religious context (Crichton) and the contemporary cultural climate (Hughes) in which exploration of worship must now occur. I could have gone further to offer more divergent definitions even from Christian writers. My point, however, is not to reach a conclusive definition of worship, or even Christian worship. I want simply to relate these

---

[30] This is a common fault of much 'theology and the arts' discussion, for reasons indicated in P. Coates, *Cinema, Religion and the Romantic Legacy*, 9. Coates agrees with Jasper's belief (see D. Jasper, 'On Systematizing the Unsystematic', in C. Marsh and G. Ortiz (eds.), *Explorations in Theology and Film*, 244) that Hollywood has little to offer theological discussion. I return to this point in Chapter 5 below.

[31] J.D. Crichton, 'A Theology of Worship' in C. Jones, G. Wainwright and E. Yarnold (eds.), *The Study of Liturgy*, 5.

[32] Gray, 'Worship', 762.

[33] Hughes, *Worship as Meaning*, 152–3, 160.

characterisations of worship with the sense in some forms of film-watching of being 'taken out of oneself'. I present these working definitions of worship as a background against which to consider a significant characterisation of the film-watching experience deriving from a film studies perspective: that offered by Ed Tan and Nico Frijda. In this way, we shall be in a better position to examine whether entertainment and worship do indeed overlap.

Tan and Frijda's exploration of the role of sentiment in film-watching will prove vital to my argument throughout this book.[34] Noting that 'contemporary research in the psychology of emotion on the subject of sentimental emotion is scarce',[35] they examine a number of basic patterns of response to films which can be classified under the heading of 'sentiment'. The overall tenor of responses takes the form of 'helplessness and submissiveness in the face of the overwhelming'.[36] They also suggest recurring filmic themes which consistently arouse a sentimental response. These are 'the separation-reunion theme, the justice in jeopardy motive, and the awe-inspiration theme'.[37]

The separation-reunion theme taps into fundamental psychological processes to do with attachment and separation. Parent-child relationships are especially significant here, though brother-sister and friend-friend relationships may function in a similar way. In discussing the psychological impact of filmic explorations of this theme, Tan and Frijda refute reductive psychoanalytic accounts of what films are 'doing'. They note Western culture's difficulty, in post-Freud times, in handling issues of attachment, since independence has become the assumed goal of the would-be autonomous human being. Aroused sentiment to do with attachment or dependence which results in the shedding of tears, especially by men, is seen as negative, a psychological weakness. Rather than crying at the cinema being considered an instructive, developmental, and quite normal human experience in response to scenes of separation and reunion, such a response can be devalued or explained away. One might add to this that any film provoking such a response could then equally be (negatively) characterised as a mere 'tear-jerker', or filed away in the genre of 'romantic comedy'.[38]

---

[34] Tan, E.S. and Frijda, N., 'Sentiment in Film Viewing' in C. Plantinga, C. and G.M. Smith (eds.), *Passionate Views: Film, Cognition, and Emotion*, 48–64

[35] Tan and Frijda, 'Sentiment in Film Viewing', 52.

[36] Tan and Frijda, 'Sentiment in Film Viewing', 55.

[37] Tan and Frijda, 'Sentiment in Film Viewing', 55.

[38] Potentially, therefore, not receiving considered treatment in some quarters of film studies, and certainly not the attention of serious theologians. For a counter to such a tendency, see e.g. Lyden, *Film as Religion*, chs. 8–9.

The second suggested theme, the justice in jeopardy motive, links emotional response to moral sensitivity. Here, the viewer identifies with a character placed in a tricky moral dilemma. In the context of a film-watching experience, however, the moral dilemma does not simply become an ethical case study for the viewer to consider. Characters in the midst of such dilemmas evoke viewers' sympathy and lure them in different ways into emotional responses. In addition to moral complexity, viewers are thus required to work with their own emotional responses. As Tan and Frijda note, the theme of self-sacrifice is also often present. They conclude: 'Perhaps the idea of giving up oneself for the right cause is the ultimate resolution of the dramatic conflict that lies at the heart of the justice in jeopardy theme.'[39] Films featuring a 'sensitive beast figure' (e.g. *Beauty and the Beast, The Elephant Man*) are one genre in which the 'justice in jeopardy' theme is prominent. Though apparently distant from everyday experience, these films' subject matter and emotional impact work *together* in enabling (requiring?) an attentive viewer to explore a moral issue both cognitively and emotionally.

Finally, Tan and Frijda consider 'the awe-inspiration theme'. It is here where the link with worship is arguably most apparent. The first part of their exploration is worth quoting in full:

> The third theme is the least specific because it is not immediately associated with the film story's action or with an understanding of the protagonist's feelings. We will call it the awe-inspiration theme. Being in an environment in which one feels tiny and insignificant, such as a huge coliseum or a cathedral, experiencing the vastness or endlessness of a landscape or empathizing with music may provoke two kinds of emotional response. In both cases, the stimulus is appraised as larger than oneself, and it provokes a tendency of helplessness and surrender, and serious respect as the less-intensive response. On the one hand, the stimulus may be attractive and call forth fascination, a propensity for further contemplation and losing oneself in it. On the other, it may have a repellent quality, eliciting a tendency to shiver and look for shelter. Both variants of awe may be seen as sentimental in the sense that they relate to yielding.[40]

This quotation contains many insights worthy of fuller exploration. In the first place, the location of the viewer is important. Here, Tan and Frijda in fact underplay the ambiguity of the viewer's location. Being in 'a huge coliseum or a cathedral, experiencing the vastness or endlessness of a landscape' refers to the

---

[39] Tan and Frijda, 'Sentiment in Film Viewing', 60.
[40] Tan and Frijda, 'Sentiment in Film Viewing', 62.

interaction between the viewer and what is portrayed on film. Experiencing being 'tiny and insignificant' could, however, result also in part from the vastness of an auditorium in which a viewer sits.[41] A significant difference in the film-watching experience between attending a cinema and watching at home must therefore be acknowledged.[42]

Second, the coincidence of language between Tan and Frijda's account of 'the awe-inspiration' theme and Crichton's definition of worship should be noted. The 'attraction, fascination and a repellent quality' in the film-watching experience echo the awe-inspiring fascination brought about by encounter with the mystery at the heart of worship.[43] It can, of course, be argued that there is much that remains different between the two accounts. In Crichton's account, God/the Other/the Divine is assumed to be the mysterious source of worship, whom a worshipper encounters with a mixture of awe, fear and fascination. This need not in any sense by read out of, or into, Tan and Frijda's comments. Indeed, the fact that they refer to the Nazi film-maker Leni Riefenstahl's 'awe-inspiring imagery' (e.g. in *Triumph of the Will*) as an example of this theme, indicates that such awe is not without its dangerous ambiguities. It is not, however, unreasonable to suggest that when directed to positive, life-enhancing ends, awe, wonder and fascination have a common source, and that this is not simply to be equated with what humans are capable of. Awe, wonder and fascination occur in *response* to something. In this sense, the cinema is a location in which such attentive responsiveness can occur.

The third insight contained within Tan and Frijda's quotation concerns the theme of yielding. The theme of helplessness and submissiveness is recurrent throughout their study of the sentimental in film. Highlighting it here, at the point at which the similarity between the film-watching experience and worship is most apparent, touches on a crucial point. Is worship as a human activity always tapping into a sense of inadequacy or self-doubt on the part of a worshipper? The view that religion is, by definition, for the weak could be held to be confirmed by Tan and Frijda's exploration here. Only those who do not have a clear sense of their own identity as people, who long for some 'possibly idealized, paradisiac

---

[41] There is an echo here of the impact of cinemas as a buildings upon John Walsh, especially given that his experience of worship at the time was far from positive. See Walsh, *Are You Talking To Me?*, 24–5.

[42] '... (T)he very physical experience of watching a film changes from living room to cinema ...'. See Plate, 'Religion/Literature/Film', 28.

[43] A key source for exploration of worship in these terms is R. Otto, *The Idea of the Holy*.

childhood memories of being completely accepted',[44] will find
worship helpful. Again, though, Tan and Frijda's enquiries do not
inevitably lead here. Nor is this the conclusion they themselves
draw. Sentiment as an emotion relating to helplessness, submissiveness and yielding, does probably link psychologically, they suggest,
with basic feelings of complete acceptance, with roots in childhood.
But their discovery of the links between sentimentality and weeping
at the movies does not lead them to discredit or devalue either the
films which produce such sentiment, or the psychological processes
at work. On the contrary, they are to be noted and recognised as
important.

For the purposes of this book, however, some important questions to ask of worship can be drawn from the exploration of the
filmic evocation of sentimental emotions. To what extent does
worship tap into the same emotional resources? To what extent do
particular images of God help or hinder the psychological processes
at work in the correlation between emotions evoked and the sense
of 'well-being' of childhood? These are not questions which can be
addressed directly here. But they do invite the drawing of summary
reflections on this comparison between film-watching and worship.

Film fulfils a similar function to worship when it evokes emotions such as those Tan and Frijda identify. Entertainment can,
then, be like worship. Approaching films in this way may, of course,
restrict the possibility of what they can achieve. For are not films
also art? I have, however, not wanted to address the distinction
between art and entertainment simply so as to be able to explore
observations about what film in its most popular forms do to people
and what people do with film. I do not dispute that films, perhaps
art-house films especially, may be capable of much more. But the
aesthetic impact of films is less my concern than the way they function affectively. Reflection on the worship-like possibilities opened
up by the interplay between film and the affective response of
viewers becomes raw material for theology.

Film is, however, in one clear sense of the term *not* worship. A
film is not usually shown *in order* to enable people to worship.[45]
The worship which can result from the film-watching experience, in
the limited way I have identified, is but a by-product of its main
function, i.e. to entertain. Furthermore, the link between the film-
watching experience and worship is thus far confined to worship's
emotional component. The significance of the link should not,
however, be downplayed. Studies of worship (except those from

---

[44] Tan and Frijda, 'Sentiment in Film Viewing', 63.
[45] Unless it is shown, for example, by a religious group, in the context of a
'worship event', and thus contextualised as a part of worship.

more charismatic or Pentecostal sources) tend to focus too heavily on worship's cognitive and aesthetic aspects.[46] The possibility opens up, then, that the decline of interest in organised worship (and institutionalised religion generally) in the West may be related to the fact that it is *in other cultural forms* that people are finding needs met which Christian and other religious believers might more easily equate with worship. It will not do, as often happens in Christian circles, simply to say that people want 'feel-good religion'. Worship entails more than emotion. But worship will not relate to life as a whole if it does not also involve the emotions. Conversely, film-watching can be more than entertainment and may not simply be a 'feel-good experience'. People watch films such as *Schindler's List, The Pianist, Apocalypse Now, Platoon, Born on the Fourth of July,* and *JFK* for more than entertainment, and not just to get themselves educated. There is entertainment and education, but there is also more. I suggest that this critical comparison between film as entertainment and worship invites reflection on what that 'more' amounts to. By the time we reach Chapter 6 of this book, the potentially integrative function of the practice of film-watching within the structure of human living, as an 'exercise in spirituality', will become clearer. Here I wish simply to suggest that without pressing the 'more' dimension, wider culture runs the risk of impoverishment, and its cinema-goers are in danger of becoming victims of spiritual neglect.[47]

Films and Audiences in Contemporary Debate

The most common criticism of any film-theology or film-religion dialogue is that religious people simply impose their reading of the world onto films. Such religious types fail to 'take film seriously', probably misunderstand what they are interpreting and simply use films as a vehicle for purveying a view of the world reached on other grounds. Films have to be taken on their own merits as film. And the directors themselves make claims on the meanings of their films.

Though it is of course true that films need to be taken on their own terms, and their form as films needs respecting, this line of criticism of the film-theology/religion dialogue has been shown to be deficient since the rise of reader-response criticism. Reference to literature studies is not always helpful in film studies, lest films be treated as too similar to literary texts. Here, though, the comparison is useful.

---

[46] Hughes, *Worship as Meaning* is a good example of this.
[47] Marsh, *Christianity in a Post-Atheist* Age, 120–2.

Reader-response criticism has brought to the fore the way in which readers, individually and as reading communities, contribute to the task of finding and making meaning in and from 'texts' of all kinds. Though there may have been a single author of a text, and that author's intention in writing a text may even be known, this does not exhaust the possible meaning that the author's text might have. Readers bring themselves to texts, and need to offer who they are to a text in order to find meaning 'from' it (or, more accurately, in response to it).

Furthermore, even adopting a less reader-oriented way of reading, it is now clear that an author may reveal so much more about him- or herself than he or she intended. To clarify an author's intention thus becomes a very limiting goal in interpretation. A psychoanalytical reading of a text, for example, may thus disclose much more than a search for authorial intention in relation to a text suggests.

Meanings may not, though, always be hidden and in need of disclosure by psychoanalysts, or reside largely in the lives of readers. Many novelists speak of the characters they create as seeming to have lives of their own. They develop a story around the characters, and yet their own imaginations are limited. They are fully aware that readers will use their imaginations in turn in interacting with the fictional characters they create. In constructing a work of fiction, then, novelists themselves are indicating that they expect readers to 'read into' a text in order better to enjoy and understand what is written. Understanding is not confined to reading the author's mind. It is to 'think with' and 'imagine with' an author in the search of a fresh thought, insight, emotion or experience.

As far as films are concerned, the notion of authorial intention becomes very strained. Whose 'intention' is supposed to be teased out from the 'text' of the film, when screenplay writers, producers, directors, film editors have all had their say? The director's intention is the most plausible cinematic equivalent of the author's intention. But even here, the availability of 'director's cut' versions of films indicates that things are not clear. The experience of film-watching thus supports the importance of reader-response criticism. Watching a film heavily qualifies the quest for the author's intention. The experience of watching makes it clear that whatever the director intended, this is not all that the film becomes. Space is opened up for examining how a film works in its interaction with the viewer. Though it is true that novels can leave much to the reader's imagination, films can actually do more in their own right in a variety of ways (through visual imagery, sound, music and the setting of their showing).

This book therefore builds on the recognised importance of what people bring to the habit of film-watching. In this light, the offering of theological interpretations of film is not in itself a problem. The greater problem is the failure to recognise that every act of film-watching occurs within a complex interaction between film and viewer. More important than what a director intended, or what a film might seem to 'say' in any obvious sense, is how a film fulfils a range of functions in any given cultural context, including a context where religion and spirituality continue to be discussed.

In the world of film studies, Martin Barker has seen all of this very clearly. I shall draw on his insights directly in the final section of this chapter. Even whilst his own film analyses show no explicit concern for any religious or theological meaning, his 'pro-filmic' approach to watching a film relates directly to the concerns I am raising throughout this book. Building on the insights of reader-response criticism, and with a great debt to the work of David Bordwell, Barker remarks: 'Popular films ... call on available cultural competences ... emergent understandings ... repertoires of emotional response ... Our mode of participation ... is awash with elements of practical reasoning coupled with involvements and commitments ... all story-following involves audience responsiveness ...'.[48]

His pro-filmic theory is thus less concerned with identifying 'the' meaning, or even meaning as such, in or from a film. He is seeking to be true to film, i.e. not distorting what is actually presented on screen to the viewer, by looking for all sorts of cues and links within a film. The exercise is not undertaken, however, in search of some elusive authorial intention. It is a form of analysis which examines how film works in relation to the viewer: how/why does the film work in this way? What does the film as text do to the viewer by what is presented on screen? A film (as 'text') is thus not *determinative* of a viewer's response (this is far from film-textual fundamentalism). But nor can Barker be accused, in his support of a reader-response approach, of implying that a viewer somehow fills a void created by a film with whatever interpretative meaning he or she wishes. A film still makes claims and has some say in what is concluded.

Barker does, though, want to look beyond film in search of what films actually do. An appropriate analysis of film for Barker, we might say, cannot rest content with films themselves. This is not a mere fad or wish on his part. He is responding to the way things are. By generalising an argument Barker makes about one particular

---

[48] Barker, *From Antz to Titanic*, 47

film, we may say that film 'embodies a call upon audiences to feel responsibility for the past, to reconnect themselves with where they come from, to learn about themselves from what the past has left us'.[49] This is a clear argument for cinema's function in being a tradition-resourcing medium.

Barker also notes that 'we have a culture that ... discourages articulation of what popular films do to people.'[50] Many words in this simple-sounding statement are significant, as they all pertain to the struggles experienced by those who seek to foster sensible theological discussion of contemporary films. First, much in Western culture discourages *articulation* at all. It is best simply to enjoy rather than reflect. To encourage people to express and examine what a form of entertainment might be doing to them is therefore itself counter-cultural. Second, film is doing something *to* people. We are beyond the conscious and the cognitive here: films work on many levels. Third, there is significance in the word 'popular'. It is more academically acceptable to offer film analyses of 'art films' than it is to be dealing seriously with blockbusters. If Barker notes this from a film studies perspective, it is still truer in the world of theology and religious studies.[51]

Pro-filmic theory, however, is most promising in taking audiences seriously and thus in enabling religion/theology/spirituality-interested viewers to take a legitimate place in the range of viewers whose responses Barker is keen to respect. He summarises his approach like this:

> *Pro-filmic theory*, then, is that aggregate of concepts through which we can address films as constituting imaginative universes. These generate possible (sensuous, emotional, aesthetic, cognitive, social) roles for audiences to occupy. Through inhabiting these, they can construct an engagement with the film's process. In and through this process, films proffer proposals for how the imaginative universe might be brought into relation with other aspects of its audiences' lives. Pro-filmic theory therefore always reaches out beyond films themselves to the surrounding world of film production and distribution, to the histories of cinema and its role in people's lives, to different communities of response.[52]

The emphasis upon film's 'role in people's lives' is telling. Even if people go along to 'enjoy themselves' when they watch a film,

---

[49] Barker, *From Antz to Titanic*, 187.
[50] Barker, *From Antz to Titanic*.
[51] Coates, *Romantic Legacy*.
[52] Barker, *From Antz to Titanic*, 193.

matters cannot be left there. That is the basis of pro-filmic theory, and also the premise upon which the whole enterprise of the film-theology/religion dialogue is based. If this dialogue is to prove legitimate from a film studies perspective, i.e. in doing justice to film as film, then it must show how the criticism that religious people impose their worldview on unpromising material proves wholly misplaced. I demonstrate this in the following two chapters in relation to available film analyses of two recent films: *The Shawshank Redemption* and *Titanic*.

One final point: Barker concludes his book noting how little research has been undertaken into the affective dimensions of audience responses to films. He is aware, he states, of 'few if any procedures for exploring how emotional responses to film might be structured'.[53] From the perspective of film-theology/religion dialogue it would be easy to retort that this is precisely where such dialogue becomes important: Barker needs to respect religion more as one of his conversation-partners. Theology would then function as a cognitive world in relation to which emotional responses to film would be structured. We are, we might say, in a cultural context in which the affective aspect of life is recognised to be important ('how does it feel?'), spirituality is seen as a good thing yet organised religion is in decline, and in which assistance is needed in the cognitive structuring of emotions. What are people to do with their emotions? Where do they lead? What do they teach us? My contention is that film-watching is a crucial element in contemporary life which opens up the emotional life for scrutiny. I contend further that theology helps in the task of critical reflection upon the emotional life and is itself challenged as to its purpose in the process.

A word of caution is needed, however. If religion, theology and spirituality can all come to bear in the examination of how people can structure their emotional responses to film (recognising that emotional responses are not the only responses to film), it would be unwise to imply that by 'getting religion' all would be well. The disputes in the film-theology/religion dialogue itself, and the widespread neglect in film studies of religious studies as an interdisciplinary partner, indicates that discussion will not be easy. Furthermore, religions tend to be quite poor in their explicit appreciation of popular culture. But that Barker's approach exists at all is an indication of what is possible.

I turn, in chapters 3 and 4, to two extended studies which show that the reception of popular films can open up discussion of how the concerns, beliefs and practices of religion, theology and

---

[53] Barker, *From Antz to Titanic*, 194.

spirituality must inevitably be recognised as an aspect of Western culture, even in a so-called secular age. My approach is to begin not within the realm of religious studies or theology, but to begin from the work of film critics and film analysts. In this way, the integrity of a film, and evidence about audience responses, set the agenda. Imposition of a religious agenda, or attention merely to identifiably religious films, is far from view.

Case-Study B

The Films of Robin Williams

Robin Williams 'has a claim as the biggest box-office attraction from the mid-1980s: since 1986, he has starred in seven films that have each taken more than $100m at the US box-office, putting him ahead of Tom Hanks ... and Tom Cruise'.[1] The roles he plays are often 'sentimental', the characters, until recently, usually 'ingratiating'.[2] This mixture of success and sentiment merit closer examination.

Williams has starred in over thirty films since his big-screen debut in *Popeye* in 1980, providing a starring voice rather than a full personal presence in a number of films (e.g. *Aladdin* 1992). In many films, Williams has played a liberating character. He has been the unusual individual able to unlock others. In *Good Morning, Vietnam* (1987) he plays a disc-jockey whose unconventional style challenges military authority whilst being well received by the soldiers who actually bear the brunt of the task of fighting the war. In *Dead Poets Society* (1989) he plays an English teacher who goes against the school's tradition in the style and content of his teaching, as he seeks to unlock the potential of his pupils. *Awakenings* (1990) and *Patch Adams* (1998) both find Williams playing medical roles, offering unusual and controversial methods of treatment and care. In *The Fisher King* (1991), he is a tramp who brokers a former disc-jockey's search for salvation.

Another group of characters Williams has played are what may be termed 'man-child roles': *Hook* (1991), *Jumanji* (1995) *Jack* (1996).[3] To this group of characters, in each of which Williams plays a child's role as an adult (Peter Pan in *Hook*, Alan Parrish in *Jumanji*) or a child whose body ages too quickly (*Jack*), can be added other films which find Williams exploring parent-child

---

[1] J. Walker (ed.), *Who's Who in the Movies*, 490.
[2] Walker (ed.), *Who's Who in the Movies*.
[3] I owe the term, and exploration of its applicability to much of Williams' work, to A. Dougan, *Robin Williams*.

relationships – *The World According to Garp* (1982), *Mrs Doubtfire* (1993), *The Birdcage* (1996) and *Father's Day* (1997) – or playing a character haunted by earlier life experience, in *The Best of Times* (1986).

One film links these two character patterns together: *Good Will Hunting*. In his 1997 Oscar-winning performance as the therapist Sean Maguire, Williams continues the trend of playing liberating figures. Here, he helps a troubled young man (played by Matt Damon) to deal with his past, whilst recognising and affirming his gift for mathematics. The relationship between the characters played by Williams and Damon, which forms the heart of the film, is complex and powerful. The therapy is not wholly one-way: Maguire grows too. Parent-child dynamics inevitably overshadow the therapeutic relationship. It is perhaps not surprising that Williams was able to produce such a striking performance given the patterns of previous roles.

More recently, Williams has begun to move beyond these two basic patterns and beyond comic roles. Though *One Hour Photo* (2001) retains an interest in the exploration of family relationships, Williams plays a darker, sinister character, Seymour Parrish, who becomes obsessed by a family whose photographs he develops. In *Insomnia* (2001) Williams is a prime suspect in a thriller. Though Williams did first play an unsavoury character in 1991 (in *Dead Again*), both of these roles mark a significant departure from most of his work.

It would not, however, in my view, be right to say that these more recent roles add a fresh complexity to the roles Williams is playing. It is more accurate to say that Williams has always been playing complex roles. The complexity has simply been hidden by the apparent sentimentality of films in which he has starred. The liberating figures he has played have not lacked complexity, either in terms of their inner coherence or their impact. John Keating's teaching methods in *Dead Poets Society* both liberate and drive one student to suicide. The character of Parry in *The Fisher King* was a demanding role, requiring Williams to portray a man driven to the point of madness following the shooting of his wife. The therapist Maguire in *Good Will Hunting* is also not an untroubled man.

What is to be made of this range of roles? What would a regular watcher of Robin Williams films have encountered through being a fan of his work? Two motifs stand out. First, a viewer might note an apparent preoccupation with the theme of redemption. Characters in Williams' films are not simply in a moral dilemma or predicament. They often suffer some form of deep psychological constraint, or find themselves in an oppressive setting. Williams is often the character who brings about release. In this respect, one might conclude that Williams regularly plays characters capable of being understood as 'Christ figures': figures who enable the transformation of others.

The roles Williams has often played clearly utilise Williams' off-screen persona: a highly energetic and creative comic. Williams' own personal life has not been without its troubles, however. He struggled with addictions to alcohol and cocaine at points in his life. He underwent therapy in order to enable him to handle the ending of his first marriage. His capacity to play fragile or complex characters is therefore not based on creative imagination alone. Whether the liberating figures he has portrayed may be deemed Christ figures could thus be challenged through respect for the fragility evident in many of the roles.

A better term than 'Christ figure' for the interpretation of many of Williams' roles, however, may be that of 'wounded healer'. The term 'wounded healer' has become widely used in pastoral theology and counselling as a description for a therapeutic attitude to be adopted by a counsellor.[4] The term reminds counsellors that they are themselves always only partially healed of their own forms of brokenness and failure, even when in the role of the 'helper'. It is because they have addressed and know how to live with their own failure and fragility which enables them to help others. This applies directly to the skill and creativity which Williams is able, through acting, to bring to the roles he plays.

A second prominent motif throughout Williams' work is a concern to explore 'family values'. Williams has starred in many 'family films', i.e. films made for families with young children to watch together. He has also acted in films that explore family relationships, not always in conventional ways. *The Birdcage* is the clearest example of this, leading Williams himself to comment:

> Lots of Americans look at San Francisco and say 'That place is crazy' … But I used to live at 19th and Castro, and it's a neighbourhood. Yeah, there are a lot of gay men and gay women, but it has the same values as your neighbourhood. They want peace and quiet. They want to live their lives, and they do have children from previous marriages, artificial insemination, a hundred different ways. It's family oriented. People don't acknowledge it, but that's the reality.[5]

---

[4] The term derives from Henri Nouwen (H. Clinebell, *Basic Types of Pastoral Care and Counselling: Resources for the Ministry of Healing and Growth*, 418–19).

[5] Cited in Dougan, *Robin Williams*, 274.

Many of Williams' films thus offer an unusual perspective on family values. Though sentimental in tone, such a film as *Mrs Doubtfire* provides an unconventional entry point to questions about parent-child and husband-wife relations. Taken as a whole, the films in which he has starred do not simply promote an easy, presupposed pattern for family living. They ask hard questions about how people grow and develop, both in relation to primary relationships within families, and to other relationships which develop through education, work and life events.

This case-study of the films of Robin Williams is presented not merely to highlight features of his own work. It functions as an example of 'star studies'. A feature of the film-watching experience is the attraction of big names in films. A viewer who therefore watches all the films of a major star is exposed to a particular style of film. Very versatile stars (e.g. George Clooney, Anthony Hopkins, Nicole Kidman, Meryl Streep) may present cinema-goers with a broader scope of material by which to be provoked and to enjoy than those who play a more limited range of characters (e.g. Hugh Grant, Arnold Schwarzenegger). The range of subject matter or types of film are not, however, readily to be systematised. Many factors influence actors' choices of films. But as this brief study of a selection of Robin Williams films indicates, a habit of film-watching influenced by reference to a star may lead to repeated exposure to common themes. When taken alongside the emotional and aesthetic dimensions of the film-watching experience, such exposure may prove formative for a viewer.

3

What Films Do To People (I): *The Shawshank Redemption*

... when I was asked to write and present a Channel Four documentary to accompany a screening of *The Shawshank Redemption*, it was toward the audience reaction that I turned my attention, convinced that there must be *some* reason why such an apparently innocuous film was having such a profound effect on so many disparate viewers. It was during the course of making that documentary ... that I first encountered the quasi-religious interpretation of Frank Darabont's movie which ... may go *some* way toward explaining its extraordinary appeal.[1]

These words appear in the prologue of Mark Kermode's British Film Institute study of the 1994 film *The Shawshank Redemption*. His initial reaction to the movie's popularity is in part understandable. On first viewing it can seem to be a prison yarn, with some stock characters and many typical features of the prison genre, but scarcely a life-changing work of art. It presents one version of organised religion, in the form of the Christianity of the prison warden, Samuel Norton (Bob Gunton), but this does not appear a dominant motif in the film, despite the film's title. The contrast between Norton's repressed and hypocritical (almost film stereotypical) form of Christianity and the other senses of freedom/redemption/liberation with which the film deals merely undercut the warden's version of Christian faith.

Yet the film had an extraordinary impact on its viewers. Opposite the frontispiece of his study Kermode quotes from Morgan Freeman and Tim Robbins, the leading actors in the film, and from director Frank Darabont. For example, Robbins says:

There isn't a day when I'm not approached about that film, approached by people who are so ... thankful, who say how important that film was to them, and how many times they've seen it: twenty, thirty, forty times ...[2]

---

[1] Kermode, *Shawshank Redemption*, 8.
[2] Related interviews are contained in the Channel 4 documentary *Shawshank: The Redeeming Feature*.

The Shawshank Redemption thus serves as an example of a recent film which can stand up to scrutiny as a good film, but whose impact takes it well beyond the judgments of film critics. The challenge which Kermode takes up is to offer an interpretation of the film which makes sense of, and does justice to, the response it received. For that response was clearly based on more than merely the fact that people enjoyed it.

The Shawshank Redemption is based on a novella *Rita Hayworth and Shawshank Redemption* by Stephen King, first published in 1982. The story centres on the relationship between two prisoners, Ellis Boyd Redding (known as 'Red', played by Morgan Freeman) and Andy Dufresne (Tim Robbins). At one level it is a prison break-out movie, a simple story about how one character (Dufresne) who is legally innocent, is incarcerated, alongside another who is legally guilty. The two are from different social, economic and racial backgrounds and much of their character development relates to such aspects. They both get out of prison in the end, by different means, and there are a number of sub-plots interweaving with this main storyline, to one of which (the hypocrisy and fate of the warden) I have already referred.

One possible reading of the film begins from the observation that the 'redemption' of the title may be more about Red than Dufresne. Unlike Brooks Halten (James Whitmore), a character in the film who is released from prison only to commit suicide on being unable to cope with his freedom, Red is released and manages to survive. The three parole hearings which Red experiences create a framework for the film. The first two are almost identical, and unsuccessful. The third, when he actually lets the shutters down, and reveals the extent to which he has understood himself, forms the grounds for his final release. Kermode regards the third parole hearing as 'Freeman's best scene in the film, the point around which the drama truly pivots, the real moment of "redemption" promised in the title'.[3]

David Thomson's comments on the film are less positive:

> ... who or what is redeemed here – in the parable-like prison called Shawshank? Is it the central figure, Andy (Robbins), wrongfully

---

[3] Kermode, *Shawshank Redemption*, 80. The significant use of humour in the way that the third parole hearing is resolved, i.e. the fact that the audience is made to laugh in the context of watching a film which is otherwise 'full of instances of pointless brutality, poignant tragedy and grim irony, but very little humor' is explored by D. Eitzen 'The Emotional Basis of Film Comedy' in C. Plantinga and G.M. Smith (eds.), *Passionate Views: Film, Cognition and Emotion*, 84–99.

convicted, yet finding a kind of fulfilment and understanding in prison? Or is it just that our mixed feelings about prison are cosily reconciled – so that we can disapprove of the system, while telling ourselves that it never quite kills hope or humanity? … the movie unwinds slowly, and not without pleasures. But I think there's a lot of humbug and wishful thinking at its core.[4]

So what do we have here? We find two well-known contemporary film critics trying to get to grips with a hugely popular film, in the title of which is a term (redemption) that invites theological exploration, yet the precise meaning of which is left relatively ill explored in the film itself. Indeed, the distinction between 'redemption' and 'rehabilitation' is scarcely examined, even though the latter is more verbally explicit in both novella and film. Why redemption? Is it some simple joke – the redemption of Red? Stephen King himself does not seem altogether clear. In his introduction to the shooting script of the film King offers no great insight as to why he gave the short story the title he did. It is surprising that the term 'redemption' remained in the film title. King himself knew that it was unlikely that any major film-backer would take up the challenge, though King was happy to let Darabont try.[5]

There may be three reasons why the term remains in the title, even if its meaning is explored explicitly neither in the novella nor the film:

1. It is assumed that the term still has some cultural currency.
2. The term will not actively put people off (or at least Tim Robbins' and Morgan Freeman's presence in the film would override any reservations on the part of film-goers).
3. There is a sense in which it relates more directly to the story's content than even the writer or director fully acknowledge or explore.

Thomson and Kermode are, at any rate, reacting very differently to the resulting film, and engage with different assumptions and at different depths with the notion(s) of redemption contained in the film. For Thomson, the redemption motif is simply unclear. His implication is that to explore it too closely would be to read in too much. Kermode, by contrast, makes what he calls the 'quasi-religious' or 'quasi-theological' aspect of the film central to his interpretation.[6] Importantly, this interpretation results from his

---

[4] In a comment on the film in *The Independent* newspaper on the occasion of one of its showings on British TV.

[5] F. Darabont, *The Shawshank Redemption: The Shooting Script*, xii.

[6] Kermode, *Shawshank Redemption*, 8, 14.

respect for audience response. A question arising from this present book is why Kermode cannot simply say 'religious' or 'theological' here.

My own position in response to this film-critical debate concerning *The Shawshank Redemption* can be summarised thus. The film deals directly with what Christian theology has called 'salvation', but deals with it incompletely. It does not satisfactorily address the communal dimension of salvation. Nor does it consider the basis upon which any forgiveness received might be received. There is much 'cognitive filling' needed, i.e. reflective development of what actually happens in and as a result of Red's experience . This would extend considerably what the film presents. The film gives enough cues, however, to indicate that it is explicitly willing to enter this field of interpretation. It is not illegitimate to offer such a theological reading of the film; far from it. The cues are all over the place. They are both cognitive and emotional, a fact which will prove crucial to my overall thesis in this book. What is more, Kermode's evidence satisfies Barker's concern to respect what the film actually does to audiences who see it (the 'cultural competences ... emergent understandings ... (and) repertoires of emotional response ...' to which Martin Barker refers).[7] The theological response to, and exploration of, the film is thus legitimated not only because of its subject matter but because of what the film does to people, and what people do with it. From this perspective, I suggest, interpreters of the Christian theological tradition are invited (compelled?) in turn to consider *The Shawshank Redemption* as a contemporary theological resource.

Salvation in *Shawshank*

I suggest that *The Shawshank Redemption* offers four images of salvation. The first is what may be termed *secularised salvation*. This is the simple fact of Andy's escape from the prison. As a central feature of the story and a key feature of the genre of prison film in which *The Shawshank Redemption* locates itself, this view of salvation as escape need attract no religious interpretation at all. Andy Dufresne gets out and gets free: it is as simple as that. Religious motifs which might suggest anything different – Dufresne emerging from the shit-filled drain in order to escape, arms outstretched in crucifix-form, for example – may merely be visual teasing. However, the emotional power of the responses to other scenes in, and aspects of, the film suggest that the implicit and explicit

---

[7] Barker, *From Antz to Titanic*, 47, cited in Chapter 2 above.

religious motifs should be taken further. Even if this first, secularised form of salvation, proves the least significant in the film and the
visual allusion a stock religious motif, there is much more worth
exploring.

The second version of salvation within the film is *salvation as the
receipt of forgiveness.* This is linked to Red's parole hearings and
ultimate release, and is evident in the clear shift between Red's
responses to the review of his sentence in the first two hearings, and
his response to the third. Red's dropping of the phrase 'God's
honest truth', which he used in the first two hearings to convince the
panels that he had fully recognised the scale of his crimes, proves
profoundly ironic. It is when he lets even the religious patter disap-
pear that he reveals to the third parole panel what he has actually
discovered about himself. He cannot atone for what he has done.[8]
He took a life. He needs forgiving in a context in which he cannot be
forgiven by those he has wronged. Yet he reveals by the realisation
that he cannot atone for his actions that he can live in the light of
being released from the crushing burden of guilt. When he earlier
attempted to disguise the guilt he felt, he only revealed how much it
still shaped him. The theological irony of his dropping the religious
patter is that it is in ceasing to 'talk religious' that he reveals his recognition of what Christians call the receipt of the forgiveness of
God. This is evidenced in the extent to which he can accept himself
and the consequences of his action, and resolve to live a reformed
life, in full knowledge of continued frailty.

The power of this particular version of salvation within the film
is especially strong. Not only is it Freeman's best scene, it could be
argued as the truly central scene in the entire film. It is, I suggest, the
scene which focuses the reasons why the film can be so existentially
helpful to viewers, and thus why Robbins, Freeman and Darabont
continue to have appreciation expressed to them. In both film and
theological studies perspective, however, it is crucial that this scene
works this way in the context of the film neither because Red says
'I'm saved' nor because the scene reflects on the meaning and significance of guilt, atonement, forgiveness and redemption. It works as
a mechanism for the exploration of, and even participation in, the
experience of salvation for at least three reasons.

First, the viewer brings parallel experiences of feeling guilty and
needing forgiveness to the scene. These need in no way be as
extreme as Red's experience of guilt (as a murderer). But nor need
they be merely a collection of small moral misdemeanours. Guilt
appears to be part of the human condition. Dealing with guilt is

---

[8] Kermode, *Shawshank Redemption,* 80.

itself an aspect of moving towards fuller humanity. Salvation is not, then, to be understood solely in moral terms. It is an existential matter.

Second, we should note that Red is the narrator throughout the film. Though the film is essentially about Red and Andy, it is Red's story that we get. The film's entire framework, then, prepares the viewer to see the events described primarily through Red's eyes. This shapes the narrative to a large extent. But it does much more than this: it prepares viewers to live Red's emotional experiences with him.

Third, the film is preparing viewers emotionally in many other ways than via this narrative device for the emotional release supplied by this scene.[9] The two failed parole hearings mean we have lived through Red's disappointment. Despite being a murderer, Red is clearly a 'likeable guy' and it is not hard for viewers to empathise with him. The level of brutality within the prison intensifies a viewer's sense that this is a place which one needs to escape from.

This second form of salvation – as receipt of forgiveness – is thus pivotal in the film. It must be explored cognitively to establish its full range of meanings and significance. To leave exploration of it at the cognitive level, however, would be to miss both how the film works, and how salvation takes shape in human experience.

The third image of salvation is contained within the ending of the film. This is idealised salvation: *salvation as transcendent utopia*.[10] Red and Andy escape to Zihuatenejo in Mexico to begin, as far as we can tell, a boat business. All, it is implied, will be well. It is sunny there. This is heaven: heaven on earth.

A fourth possible understanding of salvation presented by the film is more implicit, but potentially no less important: *salvation as freedom from structure/s*. This view is implied within the third understanding, but also links with the implied critique of Warden Norton's version of Christianity throughout the film. Norton's religion is rigid, constraining, bound up with hypocrisy. 'True religion' (by implication) will be beyond all this. It may be more 'material' (this-worldly) than the supposed spiritual salvation of Norton's religion. For Andy, salvation lies within the Bible rather than in the soul: it is hidden in his copy of the Bible in the form of the rock hammer with which he will dig his tunnel to freedom. For Red and

---

[9] On the significance of this third parole hearing having a humorous climax – when the 'Accepted' stamp is thumped down on the parole form after Red's tirade against the parole panel, see Eitzen 'Emotional Basis'. That this scene provides emotional *release* in the context of the mood the film creates, and the emotions it arouses, is, of course, important.

[10] Kermode, *Shawshank Redemption*, 67–9.

Andy together, salvation lies in Mexico, outside of the prison's (and the USA's) constraining influence. But it is clearly envisioned in as structurally free terms as possible.

One final aspect of notions of salvation in the film deserves comment, though it is not a road I shall choose to follow: is Andy being presented as a saviour (Christ), or at least priestly, figure?[11] Though the answer must, I think, be 'yes, in many ways', I am not at all sure that focussing on this aspect of the film's handling of the topic of salvation is the most fruitful way to read the film and its impact theologically. For one thing, the quest for Christ figures in literature and film is a tired (and sometimes tiresome) pastime, so that any character who helps another to come to some major realisation about themselves can be seen as salvific, and thus Christ-like. This borders on triteness. For another, to focus on individual figures in their Christ-likeness frequently fails to do justice both to the dynamic of a salvation experience, and to the way in which Christian tradition itself deals with the meaning of Christ. It is often accepted that Christ is present incognito. Though in non-theological perspective such an interpretative strategy can sound like an admission that 'Christ' is merely a name for a basic human experience, this far from follows. But searching for Christ figures is not, I suggest, the best way to support a conviction that reference to 'Christ' names a reality, rather than simply provides a language.

The Limitations of *Shawshank* Salvation

To identify four understandings of salvation at work in *The Shawshank Redemption* is not, however, to say that all are neatly expounded, fully explored or theologically satisfactory. In offering critique, I must also stress that I seek not simply to identify where the understandings do not square up with a straightforward, orthodox Christian theology.[12] I use insights from Christian theology to examine what the film and its impact produce. This is as much about critically assessing the cultural function of the film as it is about exploring a theological theme. My purpose, in short, is not merely to develop Christian theology, even though the critical dialogue enables this to happen. Furthermore, I shall not address each of the four understandings in turn, but raise critical questions which cut across the understandings examined.

---

[11] Kermode, *Shawshank Redemption*, 56–61, 68, 72–6.

[12] For one thing, a 'straightforward, orthodox Christian theology' may not exist. But that is not my main point here. I am merely indicating that I am not setting up a simple Christian checklist to see how well the film scores.

The first limitation of *The Shawshank Redemption*'s views of salvation is the extent of its individualism. Though it is true that any sense of release from any oppressive burden (physical, emotional, spiritual, material) needs to be experienced individually to be effective, there are always communal dimensions to the experience too. A person released from, or at least being able to live with, some psychological burden from their past (in the latter case therefore being released from its oppressiveness) is released into new opportunities for fuller relationships. In strictly material terms, those whose (financial) circumstances improve at least have the opportunity to participate more fully in wider forms of social living.[13]

Understandings of purity, impurity and shame differ across cultures, but are pertinent here. In cultural and social-psychological terms, salvation is bound up with patterns of inclusion and exclusion. Identification of what one needs releasing from is related to beliefs about who can be 'accepted'. In the Gospels, as recent research has emphasised, the stories of healing surrounding the figure of Jesus of Nazareth are accompanied by an emphasis on the restoration of people to their previous patterns of communal living. Lepers, even if healed, would not have rid themselves of the marks of their leprosy. Their salvation was as much a social matter as an individual physical affair.

The historical distance and cultural differences between first-century Palestine and the West in the present must not be underestimated. But the common point is clear: there are social dimensions to salvation. The unsatisfactory ending of *The Shawshank Redemption* highlights why it is important to respect this insight. The absence of respect for social salvation affects a viewer's reception of *The Shawshank Redemption's* third understanding of salvation (as transcendent utopia). The happy ending which the escape to Zihuatenejo portrays leaves unexplored the practical consequences of that escape. There are no commitments. Red and Andy apparently need to relate to no one but each other. The possible response 'but it's only a film' is itself unsatisfactory from the point of view that the ending's inadequacy *within the film's own terms* leaves the viewer aesthetically cheated. The film has, in other words, already

---

[13] This is not, of course, the same as saying that all financial gain or material improvement is intrinsically good, or that lack of material wealth indicates spiritual poverty. The contrary is often the case. But Christianity has not been very good at assessing the value of material wealth and possessions before God, despite its commitment to belief in an incarnate God. This may be because those who have much have usually been the ones articulating Christianity's theology with insufficient reference to, or experience of, those who have little.

shown its preparedness to look at some of the complexities and depth of the process and cost of 'release', through the contrast drawn between Brooks Hatlen and Red. Brooks' suicide is a stark reminder of the potential cost of salvation to the one who experiences it, in whatever form it takes. The absence of a social location within which that experience of salvation can be grasped and developed will prove life-threatening. Such aesthetic dissatisfaction functions, then, as a trigger for critical reflection on the film, which can include theological exploration.[14]

A second limitation of the film's approach to salvation overlaps with this. The 'cold simplicity' of the ending relates to a second unsatisfactory undercurrent operating throughout the film.[15] One of the reasons why Norton's Christianity can so easily be criticised is because his religion represents structural restriction. The institutional oppressiveness linking his role (warden of the prison) with his spirituality (hypocritical anyway, but designed to keep himself and others in check) has to be overcome. The implication throughout is that true salvation, true religion, true spirituality will be release from such structural oppressiveness.

Recognition of a social dimension to salvation, however, also raises the messy prospect of having to relate to others. Such relatedness is an aspect of 'real life' and thus no credible version of salvation can avoid it. Salvation cannot become so inward as to amount to the avoidance of relationship, however spiritual it be, and however individually it must be experienced. This means, in turn, that the structuring of relationships cannot be avoided either. Salvation may enable people to envision the prospect of enemies becoming friends, once people recognise that all are equal under God, that all need some kind of forgiveness, that all need releasing from something. But in the meantime, people live within friendships, families, work groups, community groups, and religious groups, all of which create fraught tensions. It is within these imperfect communities that all human life is lived. The fourth understanding of salvation in the film (freedom from structures) only works, then, because 'salvation as transcendent utopia' has no need to give thought to structures. The boat business in Mexico will have to deal with questions of investment,

---

[14] The aesthetic dissatisfaction I am expressing here differs from that voiced by Kermode, *Shawshank Redemption*, 85–6, who finds 'a beach and a boat' far too tame for a view of heaven or hope. I agree. But given that 'a beach and a boat' *is* presented and the film is thus offering images of salvation/redemption which are not solely other-worldly, then to fail to develop the 'this-worldly' salvation sells the viewer short.

[15] The term 'cod simplicity' is Kermode, *Shawshank Redemption*, 86.

cash flow crises, taxation, paperwork and employment legisla-
tion. But these are not brought into view. The ending thus under-
mines other important aspects of the film, not least its emphasis
on physicality, the time factor in relationships, and the fact that
relationships happen in a wider context.

In Christian theological perspective, to be developed more fully
such a critique would lead to critical reflection on the meaning of
'church'. Ultimately, 'church' is nothing but the attempt to address
in concrete terms the question of what form of human community
might make possible the living of life in the light of salvation. In no
sense, however, should any easy appeal to 'church' become the
answer to the questions that the film opens up. The critique offered
is more basic than this: it suggests why Christianity is so often pre-
occupied with models and forms of church, because there is no
escaping the fact that human beings need structures within which to
live and move and have their being. Sociologists confirm this even
before theologians. Between the inadequate individualism of the
film's models of salvation, and Christianity's ever-present tendency
to talk too quickly and lazily of 'church' lies a challenge to both,
therefore: what form of understanding of human community
should be sought?[16]

A third limitation of *The Shawshank Redemption's* view of salvation relates directly to Red's third parole hearing. Does Red really
'repent' and does this matter? One group of viewers to which I
showed the film stressed very strongly that he does not actually say
sorry for what he has done. There is still defiance in his words, even
whilst he has changed markedly from the first two hearings. Regret
is expressed ('There's not a day goes by I don't feel regret ...'). But
his helplessness suggests both that he cannot be forgiven, and that
there is not much point in his trying to express this regret in the form
of an apology or remorse. ('So you go on and stamp your form,
sonny, and stop wasting my time. Because to tell you the truth, I
don't give a shit.')

The question for viewers is whether we are to take Red at his
word. Does he really not care? What is contained within the regret?
Kermode clearly sees the moment of redemption for Red in the

---

[16] Christianity's own answer to this question would be 'the reign of God'.
This is sometimes also individualised ('reign of God is within you'). It must
also be acknowledged that the reign of God is a vision, which the church
seeks to embody in concrete form, and not a blueprint for any specific
model of human community. Furthermore, despite Christianity's inevitable prioritising of the church as a form of human community that seeks to
reflect the reign of God, it does not claim an exclusive role for the church in
this regard.

moment when he 'finally accepts that he cannot save himself'.[17] In my view, it is inaccurate to claim that there is no repentance on Red's part. But this conclusion is only possible because of a complex interaction between screen character and viewer which is at once cognitive and emotional. Red does not say he repents. His regret, though, will find an echo in any deep experience of regret summoned up in the viewer. An emotional bond between screen character and viewer enables a viewer to 'see' that there is a cry for forgiveness behind the words spoken. In turn, an effective response to what the film offers via this emotional interaction will only result when the film's reception is located within a wider cognitive framework in which key concepts such as redemption, salvation, liberation and atonement are given substance. The question of how experiences of regret, remorse, forgiveness, together with the absolution offered by the 'Accepted' verdict of the parole panel, are to be lived and understood is posed by the emotional exchange, but remains unanswered without an appropriate cognitive framework being offered in response.

Theology is certainly hidden here. Kermode may call the film's preoccupations 'quasi-religious' and 'quasi-theological' because he cannot quite grasp that a contemporary film or film maker might be explicit in their theological concerns. My point, though, is not that Darabont is choosing to function as a theologian, or that the film is a Christian theological text. But nor is theology simply brought to the film by the viewer. Viewers bring whatever worldviews they inhabit, whether religious or not, into dialogue with the film's content.[18] The dialogue is not, as this particular interaction with *The Shawshank Redemption* reveals, simply cognitive. Nor is it a monologue disguised as a dialogue, as if insights pertinent to theological enquiry are held by only one of the dialogue partners. There is interaction here, and, as the discussion of the film has shown, it is emotional (and aesthetic) as well as cognitive. Here is the clearest example yet of what I shall draw out more fully in Chapters 5 and 6: that theology through film is in large part an exercise in the cognitive structuring of the emotional life, provoked by the multi-dimensional experience of film-watching.[19]

---

[17] Kermode, *Shawshank Redemption*, 80.
[18] This is simply filling out in relation to the world of religion Barker's point that 'there has to be some general idea about how films relate to the world beyond them: the world of politics, the wider world of culture, ideas, ideologies, the films' makers and their audiences'. See Barker, *From Antz to Titanic*, 4.
[19] Turner, *Film as Social Practice*, ch. 5.

The *Shawshank* Challenge to Christian Theology

If the dialogue really is two-way, though, then the film has things to say to Christian theology too. I shall mention three criticisms.

First, Christianity has been insufficiently self-critical with regard to the inwardness of salvation. Whether in the form of preoccupation with guilt, or with a tendency to foster an overly introspective consciousness, Christianity has allowed some of its own understandings of salvation too easily to become a solely internalised, and individualised matter between the believer and God. A tortured soul can result. *The Shawshank Redemption* admittedly gives mixed messages with its range of salvation images, especially if the third parole hearing becomes the central image for viewers, and the stimulus for their own sense of release.[20] But locating the exploration of the theme in a prison means the film's range of understandings is grounded in a physical, material setting. Release means physically getting out. The hoped-for heaven is Mexico. Kermode's dissatisfaction with the materiality of the ending turns in the film's favour, and becomes a challenge to readings of salvation which are simply too narrowly spiritual. People 'get saved' (redeemed, liberated, released from oppression) and this salvation must matter to them here and now, or it may not be worth as much as Christianity claims.

Second, the film's views of salvation can challenge Christianity to look at the images of heaven that it has presented. Christianity has carried with it for most of its history a wide range of imagery of an after-life. All such images can be shown to have a direct impact on present life: heaven as an incentive to purity and upright living, hell as a warning against disregard of createdness and resulting immorality. Less positively, such images have proved a means of social control, or devalue present, material existence. Post-Enlightenment Christianity has often struggled to know what to do with such images and how to relate them to understandings of redemption. McDannell and Lang catalogued a wide range of images of heaven inside and beyond Christianity, concluding that '(s)cientific, philosophical, and theological skepticism has nullified the modern heaven and replaced it with teachings that are minimalist, meager and dry'.[21] Few Christians would support the notion

---

[20] Though if it could be shown through the gathering of empirical data from audience responses that it is the third parole hearing which leads viewers to keep on telling Darabont, Robbins and Freeman how liberating the film proved, this perhaps indicates the sheer power of internally-experienced salvation.

[21] C. McDannell and B. Lang, *Heaven: A History*, 352.

that all images of an afterlife must now be abandoned. It is, however, telling to find a dictionary of modern Christian thought containing neither an article nor index reference to 'heaven'.[22] *The Shawshank Redemption* may, in other words, be confronting Christianity with a weakness in the contemporary viability of its own symbol system. 'Heaven' simply does not work any more, and has not done so for some time. If it is to be refocused in terms, say, of 'the dwelling place of God' as opposed primarily to the goal of human living, then its function as a living symbol for contemporary Christian spirituality and theology will require reconsideration.

Third, Christian theology is challenged to examine more carefully how its views of salvation interweave with violence and injustice in the world. Many Christian images of salvation have focussed on inner torments. Salvation is to do with release from guilt, from the mental and emotional burden of sin and its consequences, or, more recently, from psychological blockages. Despite Liberation Theology, which has since the 1960s encouraged Christianity around the world to look more closely at the material and economic dimensions of salvation, the realities of material existence are not often brought under consideration. Forms of 'prosperity theology', according to which the acquisition of wealth is seen as a sign of God's good favour, merely accentuate the notion of salvation as escape from, or even salvation as avoidance of, what life for most people comprises.

There is no avoiding physical brutality as a key element in the plot of *The Shawshank Redemption.* Kermode highlights the point in his discussion of how the film treats male rape.[23] Within the context of a prison – an institution which exists to enable society to deal with violence – further violence follows. The film does not shirk this, and is thus graphic in its portrayal of violence as part of human living. It does, however, implicitly support the primacy of an inner experience of salvation. The telling scene here is Dufresne's illicit playing of Mozart over the warden's public address system, following discovery of *The Marriage of Figaro* in a batch of records sent to the prison. The scene provides confirmation of Dufresne's basic approach to life: no-one can take away the inner possession of hope.

The maintenance of this inner conviction itself carries the physical consequences of solitary confinement for Dufresne. Inner hope is maintained in a context of violence, and carries a punishment. Any direct parallels with Christian understandings of salvation and

---

[22] A. McGrath (ed.), *The Blackwell Encyclopedia of Modern Christian Thought.*
[23] Kermode, *Shawshank Redemption*, 21–7.

hope at this point might be to claim too much, although the recognition that maintaining Christian conviction is often costly has plenty of evidence to support it. The film's exploration of the interwovenness of salvation and violence does, however, merit emphasis in two respects. First, it challenges Christianity to own up to whether it always acknowledges the reality of physical violence in whatever context it seeks to interpret the meaning of salvation. Second, the film demands that Christianity recognise how it makes use of an image of violence (the cross) at the heart of its own symbol system. There is much recent discussion, especially emerging from feminist theologies, that challenges the way in which Christianity understands and presents its own beliefs at this point. To say that salvation comes through the cross is not the same as saying that violence is inevitable and required as a means of salvation.[24] Attention to the cross should, in fact, require Christians to confront the reality of violence in the world. This second point does, however, extend a challenge to Christians to acknowledge how the cross can too easily lead to the acceptance or sanctioning of violence in the name of Christianity.

Summary

This discussion of *The Shawshank Redemption* highlights a number of points about theology's interaction with film. In the first place, the possibility of a film's explicit interest in theological subject matter, whilst not being an identifiably religious film, is confirmed. This possibility has been the source of many contributions to the theology/religion-film dialogue. Theological reception of film cannot rest content with such links. But they can also not be denied in their importance. In this chapter, we have been able to explore religious language, critique of religion and an expressed spirituality/theology. Second, it has proved possible to focus on the impact of the film upon viewers. Deducing from the film a transformative function upon at least some of its viewers was not, in the light of the cited evidence from Kermode, an exercise in speculation. Kermode had to deal with the impact the film actually had on viewers. Third, the emotional trigger supplied by Red's third parole hearing supplied a particular insight into *how* the film is likely to have worked transformatively for many viewers. The analysis of the film thus

---

[24] Relevant writings here include J.C. Brown and C.R. Bohn (eds.), *Christianity, Patriarchy and Abuse*; R.N. Brock, *Journeys by Heart*; R.N. Brock and R.A. Parker, *Proverbs of Ashes*; J.D. Weaver, *The Nonviolent Atonement* (and the further literature discussed there).

provides the first evidence for how theological interaction with popular film may be able to work in particular alliance with such emotional triggers. Fourth, the cognitive exploration of the impact of the film upon viewers, building especially upon the emotional triggers set off, proves to be very rich. Such exploration thus indicates the value of such theological exploration as a normal feature of the reception and enjoyment of film.

4

What Films Do To People (II): *Titanic*

The literary critic Northop Frye writes:

> The Bible is clearly a major element in our own imaginative tradition, whatever we may think we believe about it. It insistently raises the question: Why does this huge, sprawling book sit there inscrutably in the middle of our cultural heritage ... frustrating all our efforts to walk around it.[1]

Titanic is scarcely the Bible, and has not even had a decade to prove itself as a 'classic', let alone a few thousand years. But on the contemporary cultural scene, it is 'just there' and there is no getting round it. Inclusion in the British Film Institute's book series of 'Modern Classics' does not make the film a classic.[2] Such treatment does, though, acknowledge the film's phenomenal success. It is the first film to have grossed a billion dollars worldwide. It was easily the most-watched film of the 1990s. Jörg Herrmann, citing Germany as an example, notes that it put *The Lion King* into second place in the list of most-viewed films, by over six million viewers.[3] It is also, to date, the most expensive film ever made. It may, possibly, be the most skillfully marketed film ever made, as its success in terms of viewing figures is surely related to a large extent to the advertising and merchandising which accompanied the film's release. The film was, however, savaged by film critics. It has been

---

[1] N. Frye, *The Great Code: The Bible and Literature*; cited in J. Riches, *The Bible: A Very Short Introduction*, 100.

[2] For the meaning of 'classic', see e.g. the extensive discussion by D. Tracy, *The Analogical Imagination: Christian Theology and the Culture of Pluralism*, ch. 3.

[3] *Titanic* was released on 8 January 1998 and was watched by 17,888,029 people by December of that year. *The Lion King* had been released on 17 November 1994 and reached 11,319,003 viewers by the same date: J. Herrmann, *Sinnmaschine Kino: Sinndeutung und Religion im populären Film*, 107.

regarded a prime example of 'market-driven film-making' and 'simple-minded entertainment'.[4] The character portrayals in the film have been described as 'execrable'. In short, artistically speaking it was felt to be not really a very good film.

Why, then, spend time on it in a book like this? I must come clean here. It was some years before I got round to watching the film. Unlike some of those people David Lubin mentions at the opening of his study of the film,[5] this was not due to any elitist decision not to consume it (and thus locate myself socially through my non-consumption). I simply did not get round to it at the time. I enjoyed watching it, but I cannot say it moved me greatly. It did, though, keep me riveted. I admired the skill which must have gone into making it. And above all, it left me wondering who it 'worked' *for*, and what can be gleaned from its success. My reasons for considering *Titanic* are thus similar to German theologian Jörg Herrmann's reasons for including it in his *Sinnmaschine Kino*: if the theology/religion-film dialogue is to locate itself appropriately within the study and critique of contemporary culture then it needs to be working with culturally significant material, including dominant examples of popular culture. It is on this basis that six of the seven films which Herrmann considers in some depth feature in the top ten list of most-watched films in Germany in the 1990s.[6] My own starting-point, however, is not the fact that this film is receiving direct treatment in the context of the theology/religion-film world.[7] It is the fact that the first review I read of the film, in a British broadsheet newspaper, took exception to the director's theology.[8] The film thus appears to function culturally in intriguing ways, which invite wider consideration.

James Cameron as Theologian: 'A New Kind of Tastelessness'?

I begin an exploration of the film, then, at the intersection between two film analysts' versions of what the film is up to. The first is the

---

[4] D. Lubin, *Titanic*, 9.

[5] Lubin, *Titanic*, 7–8.

[6] The films he considers in addition to *Titanic* are: *Pretty Woman, Jurassic Park, Forrest Gump, The Lion King*, and *Independence Day*. *Pulp Fiction* is the one exception, on the grounds that it was a film which crossed the border between popular and art house cinema.

[7] Herrmann, *Sinnmaschine Kino*, 192–208; Lyden, *Film as Religion*, 171–8.

[8] R. Gilbey, 'I've got that sinking feeling', in *The Independent*, 23 January 1998.

review by Ryan Gilbey just referred to. Gilbey is clearly offended by
what he believes Cameron's theology to be. He writes:

> It's one thing for Cameron to remind us that many people felt the
> *Titanic*'s ostentatious grandeur to be an affront to God. But when he
> speculates that this ship was doomed because a couple of teenagers
> dared to cross the class divide, he's promoting a new kind of tasteless-
> ness. The suggestion that over 1,500 real people died as a sacrifice to
> the love of two fictional characters doesn't make you swoon, it makes
> you gag. If Cameron is suffering from a God complex, then that's
> between him and his analyst – it's not a delusion which should be
> assuaged using millions of dollars and a movie camera.[9]

As a basic reading of the film, Gilbey is in one sense quite accurate.
The 'primal structural device' of *Titanic* is the 'paralleling of … two
trajectories – ship and love affair'.[10] The film interweaves Rose's
story (in two forms: past and present) with the story of the *Titanic*'s
sinking. Rose's discovery of freedom, and her sensation of 'flying'
when stretching out on the bow of the ship, coincides with the point
at which the iceberg becomes visible, and thus functions as the
major turning-point in the film.[11] The end of her relationship with
Jack, due to Jack's drowning, then also coincides with the ship
going down. Two questions arise. Is Gilbey right to conclude a
causal link between these two trajectories? Even if he is, why should
the meaning and significance of *Titanic* as a film be dependent upon
what Cameron may or may not be trying to suggest?

In response to the first question, Gilbey may, in fact, be largely
right. Lubin writes:

> … insofar as Rose symbolizes modernist sensibilities shrugging off
> sexual repression and neo-feudal marital obligation, the collision that
> her behaviour helps cause is not only with the iceberg but with the
> solidly frozen social and behavioural codes that the early twentieth-
> century modernists struggled so hard to shatter.[12]

The crucial word here is 'cause'. The assumption at work is
that there is indeed a causal link implied in the film's main two,
interlocking narratives (the sailors on the bridge are distracted by
Rose and Jack and do not see what is ahead[13]). However, to view a

---

[9] Gilbey, 'I've got that sinking feeling'.
[10] Lubin, *Titanic*, 17.
[11] Barker, *From Antz to Titanic*, 101–3.
[12] Lubin, *Titanic*, 67.
[13] This is supported by Lubin through quotation of Cameron's own words.
Lubin, *Titanic*, 66.

fictional, filmic device for making the story work as an implicit or explicit theological judgment, via the assumption of causation, is to run the risk of a kind of over-interpretation of which theological interpreters of film are often accused.[14] The function of the character of Rose within the film's own narrative in fact prevents Gilbey's interpretation being plausible. Rose is the only character in the film to undergo major development. Viewers are privileged to 'experience Rose's transformation'.[15] Through such participation, viewers are in turn invited to reflect on how they inherit and critique the living tradition(s) in which they stand. What have they done with their pasts? What have they made of their family and cultural traditions? This is, I submit, more the point of the two interlocking narratives than any implicit theological point about causation.

Gilbey might, of course, object that this interpretative strategy I am adopting simply defends God, and Cameron's view of God, against the charge of being responsible for mass, undeserved death. If there is any hint in or behind the film that rebelliousness is somehow automatically punished, as if 'that's the way the world is' (and that because God exists and is all-powerful and righteous, God is clearly to blame), then such a critique would be justified. 'The way the world is', however, indicates that such rebelliousness is not automatically punished, that if God is, and is present and at work in the world, then this is not how God is involved in social and moral change. If Cameron holds to such a view, then he is wrong, and Gilbey's charge carries great weight. Cameron would then be trading off a view of God which sees God as the instant seeker of moral rectitude through punitive means.

Like all views about God, of course, such an image is held by human interpreters operating in specific, culturally conditioned contexts. No one can wholly step outside of a specific context, even when appeals to revelation (from God) are made as a source of insight for beliefs about God. Such a strongly punitive view of God is undoubtedly still held across many religious traditions. It has a

---

[14] In other words, those interpreters who are sympathetic to theology. See e.g. the *Sight and Sound* review of Marsh and Ortiz (eds.), *Explorations*: 'It's hard not to be touched by the book's naïve desire to be now and with it, even if the total effect is as acutely embarrassing as those church services that try out rock music to fetch back the dwindling flock' (February 1998). In the light of Kermode's work in *The Shawshank Redemption*, however, it is perhaps best to call a moratorium on such critiques, accept that theological interpretation has a legitimate function, and to ask all interpreters simply to try and help each other clarify what constitutes a good, informed interpretation of a film and its reception.

[15] Barker, *From Antz to Titanic*, 103.

firm foothold in the Jewish and Christian traditions and can be deemed a 'biblical idea' in the sense that it is found there. It is not, however, a view of God's presence and action which stands up to too close scrutiny. It is not a 'biblical' notion in the sense that it constitutes the best image of God to be constructed in continuity with the general tenor of the Bible's contents. God's abhorrence at evil does not inevitably carry with it the capacity to instantly or completely eradicate that evil. In Christian understanding, for example, the belief that God has 'dealt with' evil in and through the person and work of Jesus Christ, explicitly in and through the cross, does not then mean that evil ceases to exist. The freedom granted to creation means that God must continue to accompany creation (in Christ, by the Spirit) in opposing evil.

It is, however, possible that Gilbey is wrong about Cameron. Though Cameron owns up to a causal link in film-narrative terms,[16] and though Lubin may draw important interpretative insights from the film in relation to the causal link, it is not at all clear that Cameron is making a theological point. Whether viewers actually 'see' things the way that Gilbey is suggesting would be worth checking out. Such enquiry would be a confirmation that a film's meanings lie more between a film and its reception than in either the film as film, or in the director's intent. As it is, we are faced with the strange and ironic situation that Gilbey's review may contribute to the perpetuation of an outdated God-concept, whether or not Cameron holds to the view Gilbey ascribes to him.

This film-critical starting point of a consideration of the specific film *Titanic*, then, highlights a number of intriguing aspects of the contemporary reception of film in general. First, it shows us that auteur theory (which places great emphasis upon the director's intentions in the film-making process[17]) is alive and well in film criticism. That a single theological idea supposedly held by a director should feature so prominently in the interpretation of a three-hour film within which so much is going on, is quite surprising. Current thinking about the art of interpretation places much more emphasis upon the receiver of a work of art, and on the interplay between text/film and receiver. Second, the discussion indicates the crucial cultural significance of film. It clearly matters to Gilbey that he must challenge the view which he deems Cameron to hold. As a film-critic he must, of course, do his job by being critical of the film as a film. In this regard, many of his critical points are legitimate (e.g.

---

[16] Lubin, *Titanic*, 66–7.

[17] For more on auteur theory see e.g. S. Blandford, B.G. Grant and J. Hillier, *The Film Studies Dictionary*, 16–18.

naïve characterisation, sentimentality rather than poignancy). But to address also the ideological inclinations of the director shows Gilbey's awareness of how influential this film is likely to be and this fuels his evident desire to critique what he takes to be Cameron's view. Gilbey thus clearly believes that his theological challenge is morally necessary. As I have indicated, I agree with him in his moral intent, but question both the accuracy of his interpretation of the film, and the appropriateness of this kind of discussion at this point. Third, though there is much criticism in the world of theology/religion-film dialogue around the legitimacy of finding 'links' (or analogues) between film narrative and theology/religion, here we have an example of such a procedure occurring not from the side of religion. It is profoundly ironic that were such a discussion initiated by a theologian wanting to find a *positive* image of God implicit in such a film, it would scarcely even make it to the newspaper editor's desk for serious consideration.

In all of this, however, we are still operating largely in the realm of thematic considerations. We have not begun to address either a broader range of factors on which the film invites discussion, nor, more significantly, the reasons for audience responses, i.e. how and why the film works in the way it does. To these matters we now turn.

A 'Women's Film'

What genre of film is *Titanic*? For Gilbey, it is an 'epic melodrama'. Lubin considers it 'an historical epic and a disaster movie', though 'it also derives in a major way from two other movie genres: the screwball comedy and the women's film'.[18] Lyden makes it the main focus of his chapter on 'Melodrama, Tearjerkers and "Women's Films".'[19] He writes: 'The biggest box-office success of all time can ... be considered as a women's film and a tearjerker, for although it has some of the form of an action and disaster movie, the plot is most similar to those targeted especially at women'.[20] These interpretations indicate clearly that *Titanic* functions as a 'multiple-genre' film. Whether this relates to a desire to have mass appeal need not detain us here. Artistically it could be argued that the multiple genres it inhabits make the film a confused piece of work. Clarification of a dominant genre can, though, be reached with respect to the actual reception of the film. It is along this route that I shall explore the film both as film, and in relation to its viewers.

---

[18] Lubin, *Titanic*, 37.
[19] Lyden, *Film as Religion*,164–78, esp. 171–8.
[20] Lyden, *Film as Religion*, 170.

The film clearly locates itself within the disaster movie genre by its subject-matter. It is, however, as a melodramatic love-story that it has achieved its colossal impact. The evidence of its success amongst women viewers (especially women viewers in their late teens and early twenties) is well-documented.[21] Whether, for this reason, it should also be categorised as a woman's/women's film is open to question. The entry under 'Woman's film' in *The Film Studies Dictionary* states that they are:

> Movies produced by HOLLYWOOD, particularly from the 1930s through the 1950s, featuring female STARS in STORIES about romance, family and social and domestic issues deemed important to women, and aimed at a primarily female AUDIENCE. These films tended to be MELODRAMAS involving the heroine in acts of emotional sacrifice ...[22]

There is further evaluation in the entry, through its reference to feminist studies of these films which have shown how they construct female subjectivity in such a way that the patriarchal ideology within which women lived throughout this period remained intact. The 'woman's film' thus kept women in a particular place, a confined, social space.

To identify the genre of *Titanic* as in continuity with this range of films therefore needs careful scrutiny. To express the matter starkly: if it is a 'woman's film' in the sense described above, then why is such a film being made in 1997, and why should it prove so popular? If, on the other hand, it is a film which has a particular appeal to women, but functions in an empowering rather than an oppressive way, then why call it a 'woman's film'? As Molly Haskell exclaimed in 1973: 'What more damning comment on the relations between men and women in America than the very notion of something called "the woman's film".'[23] Her remark is pertinent three decades later, and well beyond America.

My argument will run as follows. I shall suggest a number of reasons why *Titanic* comes to be called a 'woman's film'. In evaluating some of these reasons positively, I shall, however, go on to suggest that the label distorts the potential of the film to impact upon a wider range of viewers. The categorisation also stunts the possibility of broader social, psychological and cultural development, with particular reference to the relationship between women and men, and to the forms of 'knowing' which can be accessed by

---

[21] Lubin, *Titanic*, 10–12; Barker, *From Antz to Titanic*, 88.
[22] Blandford et al., *Film Studies Dictionary*, 264; capitalisation indicating cross-references.
[23] Cited in Blandford et al., *Film Studies Dictionary*, 264.

both men and women. In valuing certain aspects of how the film actually functions as film (and being critical of some other aspects), I shall conclude that the film is best considered a historical epic, in the disaster genre.

There are clear reasons why *Titanic* is categorised as a 'woman's film'. Some of the same features as were present in the women's films of the 1930s to 1950s are here: romance, a stifling engagement, a possible way out of impending marriage through a different relationship. Second, in terms of characterisation, Rose is the only character who undergoes any major character development.[24] Most other characters are 'thin', to say the least.[25] It is thus clear why women are more likely to find the film satisfying: the greater possibility of identification with its one, developing character. Third, I suspect that the film is more susceptible to receiving the label 'woman's film' for rather basic, culturally-conditioned reasons, i.e. it plays heavily on the emotions, is sentimental, and is thus to be distinguished from more 'male-oriented' (action) films. The stereotyping typical of patriarchal culture seems to remain alive and well in the world of film and film-reception.

The film does, however, step outside the classical 'woman's film' in some ways. Though stifled by patriarchal culture, Rose resists the path mapped out for her. She turns Cal down and breaks free from the marriage arranged for her. In this sense, the younger Rose

> is to be understood as a representative of modernity. She is the modern woman who was much in the news at the time of the great liner's "maiden" voyage: bold, headstrong, determined, dissatisfied with the subservient role accorded her by patriarchal tradition.[26]

In this light, it is not surprising that young women at the turn of the twenty-first century should find her a compelling role model. Does this of itself undermine the genre categorisation of *Titanic* as a woman's film, however? I do not think it does. The 'teen romance ideology' of the film,[27] the dependence on a known male star (Leonardo DiCaprio, who plays Jack Dawson, the 'stock' and rather romanticised lead male character) and the general

---

[24] Barker, *From Antz to Titanic*, 100.
[25] 'Naïve', Gilbey, 'I've got that sinking feeling'; 'paper-thin', Lubin, *Titanic*, 37; 'flat and stereotypical', Lyden, *Film as Religion*, 176.
[26] Lubin, *Titanic*, 25–6. It should also be said that feminist analysis of some of the so-called 'woman's films' highlights the strength of some of the women characters portrayed in the movies of the 1940s and 1950s. Lubin, *Titanic*, 40–3.
[27] Lubin, *Titanic*, 65.

underdevelopment of all other characters in the film all prevent *Titanic* from being an emotionally rich film. Artistically speaking, *Titanic* is too much like a 'woman's film' of the 1930s to 1950s to be a fully credible contemporary exploration either of relationships at the turn of the century, or in the present.[28]

The possible identification of *Titanic* as a 'woman's film' thus constrains its possible impact and limits the range of potential interpretations. Rather than be critical of all the reasons for its being characterised as such, however, I want to explore further the film's sentimentality and the way it seeks to construct an emotional impact on the viewer. In this way, I shall seek to show more about how the film's actual working enables it to function as 'a women's film with crossover appeal to men who want more from a movie than simply colossal effects and brutal physical action'.[29] In the process, however, I shall also have to highlight the film's deficiencies in pulling this off wholly satisfactorily.

Sentimentality is not usually considered a good thing. When the word 'sentimental' is used, it is often prefaced by the word 'merely'. The word has come to imply a falling short in the realm of the emotional. Sentimentality in literature and film means that short cuts are taken, tough and complex situations are oversimplified. Feelings do not seem to run as deep as they should, given the situations described, and plots move towards resolution a little too easily. Sentimentality is also often linked to melodrama.[30] The key to all of this is the excessiveness of the emotion aroused or displayed. More

---

[28] Bearing in mind that '(m)ovies set in the past are always, in the final analysis, *about* the present' and that *Titanic* seems to play mischievously with its anachronisms (Lubin, *Titanic*, 57–8). One filmic parallel to Titanic, in terms of its structure and even, to some extent, its central concerns vis-à-vis its lead character, is *The French Lieutenant's Woman* (1981), Karel Reisz's film, using a Harold Pinter screenplay, of John Fowles's 1969 novel. In the film, the retrojection of a woman character with modern sensibilities into Victorian culture, and the fact that the book finishes with two endings, is handled by the construction of two interlocking narratives, one set in the past, and one, the story of the actors playing the parts of the characters in a filmed version of the story, in the present. This formal parallel between the two films presses the point that, as a historical epic, *Titanic* is very much concerned with what we learn from history.

[29] Lubin, *Titanic*, 10.

[30] And in the entry in *The Film Studies Dictionary*, with 'Weepies' as well as women's films (Blandford et al., *Film Studies Dictionary*, 146). A 'Weepy' is 'a narrative work that relies on sentiment and emotional manipulation to elicit a strong, usually sad, emotional response from the AUDIENCE ... Also used synonymously with "tearjerker".' See Blandford et al., *Film Studies Dictionary*, 261.

analytically, plot takes priority over characterisation, it is clear who the heroes and villains are, and history is reduced 'to the emotional problems of individual characters'.[31] The complexity of life receives short shrift. Working with this definition, *Titanic* is undoubtedly a sentimental melodrama.

Despite its shortcomings, however, I want to defend it, and defend it both psychologically and theologically. Criticisms of sentimentality are simply too easy to make. They overlook the fact that what has come to be labelled 'sentimental' ignores an important strand of Western cultural tradition. The concept of 'sentiment' has undergone shifts in meaning from the Enlightenment to the present.[32] Nevertheless, it denotes an important dimension of human experience too easily neglected in theology, literature and film studies alike. At its simplest and most general, the term demands that attention to be given to feeling and intuition. More precisely, in the understanding offered in contemporary cognitive psychology, sentiments are 'dispositional emotions'. They are, in other words, 'attitudes one cares about'.[33]

If sentiments are, then, more than 'mere emotions', we must be prepared to acknowledge that what is termed 'sentimental' is actually touching on what is cared about most deeply. Sentimentality and melodrama in film may well go hand in hand. But emotions become excessive because of repression. Sentimental, melodramatic films can thus be seen as part of the way in which a culture deals with the collective repression of that which it finds uncomfortable. Responses to the film, in all its sentimentality, are thus responses to a filmic interpretation of what Western culture finds it difficult to handle.

In the case of *Titanic*, as we shall see in due course, it is not simply the stifling of Rose, leading to her blossoming romance with Jack, which the film addresses and sentimentalises. In a film which is '(u)nquestionably … ideological', much else is at stake. It

> proclaims to its viewers in all sorts of ways that intuitive knowledge surpasses instrumental rationality, that greed is bad, elitism wrong, freedom a virtue, self-sacrifice noble, and, above all, that true love transcends death.[34]

---

[31] Blandford et al., *Film Studies Dictionary*, 146.
[32] C. Blum 'Sentiment', in J. Yolton, R. Porter, P. Rogers and M. Stafford (eds.), *The Blackwell Companion to the Enlightenment*, 487–8.
[33] N. Frijda and B. Mesquita, 'Beliefs through emotions', in N. Frijda, A.S.R. Manstead and S. Ben (eds.), *Emotions and Beliefs: How Feelings Influence Thoughts*, 55–6.
[34] Lubin, *Titanic*, 14.

These views may be 'old-fashioned (or out-of-fashion)'.[35] They may
represent views found within 'the sentimental liberalism and popu-
lism of the Clintonian US in the late 1990s'.[36] They are undoubtedly
handled too lightly and too simplistically. But exploration of them
in such an influential film is crucially important. This is the concern
that drives Herrmann's treatment of the film, and provides his argument for why any contemporary theology cannot ignore the content
of such a film, and the manner in which its content is
communicated.

The very fact that *Titanic* is a sentimental melodrama, we might
say, is part of its main point. The way it works is part of what it is
trying to say. If there is not 'a dry eye in the house' by the time it has
finished, then it has not only succeeded in emotionally manipulat-
ing its audience, it has also in part succeeded, via that manipulation,
in getting an aspect of its message over: rationality is not everything
and male-dominated technological advance has its limits.[37] *Titanic*
handles this and other topics, however, as a historical film. It locates
its discussions historically in past and present: at the time of the
Titanic's sinking, and in the (fictional) present of the salvage crew's
attempt to work on the wreck. The film is thus commenting both on
modernity and late-, or post-, modernity through the two interweaving narratives with which it works.

In interweaving the narratives, the film seeks to recover a sense
of the value of the irrational. It does this in a sentimental way. That
the sentimentality becomes tangled up in other aspects of the film's
self-presentation and reception (as a 'woman's film') adversely
affects the film's melodramatic qualities. My point, though, is to
defend the sentimental. Despite a melodrama's tendency to over-
simplify, the sentimental has a crucial place in art in so far as it keeps
people in touch with their emotions. When art (perhaps especially
popular art) is sentimental, this may merely accentuate the absence
of attendance to the emotional dimensions of human living in so
many other realms of life (art, politics, religion). The task of interpreting the emotions aroused in either art or entertainment then
prevents their arousal being 'mere emotion', as if emotions have no

---

[35] Lubin, *Titanic*, 14.

[36] Lubin, *Titanic*, 79.

[37] That it does so through the mechanism of much technological advance
(computer-generated special effects) in a male-dominated industry is an
irony worth closer scrutiny. This also explains, perhaps, why the characterisation of *Titanic* as a 'woman's film' (as defined and constructed
largely by men) is ultimately apposite, but unhelpful as far as the film's
content is concerned.

focus. [38] As cognitive psychology shows, emotional growth occurs when the relationship between emotion and cognition is recognised and when the structuring of emotions which is always going on in daily living is acknowledged. [39]

Theology has a contribution to make here. There is little doubt that theology has often been prone to contributing to avoidance of emotion. It has been seen as a rational discipline. In the modern period, arguably, this rationalistic tendency has persisted. However, it has conducted its own struggles within itself as a discipline throughout the modern period in ways which parallel the concerns contained in the film *Titanic*. The so-called 'father of modern theology', Friedrich Schleiermacher, is, for example, known as a 'theologian of feeling'. His definition of 'feeling' is not to be equated with emotion alone, in either a vague or a technical sense. [40] Nevertheless, he is one of many challengers of unqualified rationalism in theology. Schleiermacher's conviction that the most basic human disposition is a 'feeling of absolute dependence' was no vague feeling, or unfocused emotion. Nor did it reduce theology to psychology. It was a way of speaking of a fundamental human disposition which was at once emotional and ontologically grounded (in God). [41]

---

[38] It is here where the problem of precise categorisation of film as a medium, or of specific films, proves helpful, i.e. film's ambiguity: is it art, entertainment or both?

[39] It should be acknowledged at this point that the difference between everyday speech and technical language causes complications here. 'Emotions' and 'feelings' are used interchangeably and in a very general sense in everyday speech. 'Mere emotion' as I am using it here refers to what the philosopher Noel Carroll calls 'affect' N. Carroll, 'Film, Emotion, and Genre', in C. Plantinga, C. and G.M. Smith (eds.), *Passionate Views: Film, Cognition, and Emotion*, 21. 'Emotion' when used in its more technical sense within cognitive psychology thus already implies cognitive structuring, i.e. an emotion is recognised for the kind of feeling it is, and where it is directed. There is a level of awareness present which prevents vague reference to unfocused feelings.

[40] It could be claimed that his work anticipates contemporary cognitive psychology here.

[41] Note should also be taken of Pentecostal and charismatic theologies, which are sometimes criticised for their over-emotionalism. Two observations should be made. First, the necessity for such challenges indicates a weakness of much Christian theology in the West, a weakness often ascribed to a weak doctrine of the Spirit. Second, however, Pentecostal and charismatic theologies are not known for developing an adequate cognitive/intellectual framework to accompany their proper attention to Christian experience.

A second example is that of pastoral/practical theology, one of a number of candidates for the 'Cinderella' among the theological disciplines. As the branch of theology which majors on critical reflection upon experience, and which invites people to explore their reactions and responses to situations, and to the emotions experienced within those settings, pastoral theology in particular resists the characterisation of theology as simply rational. Not surprisingly, such theology is often marginalised (behind biblical study, dogmatic, systematic, or philosophical theology).[42] *Titanic*, however, invites the theological reflection that the way the film actually works is not due merely to the issues it raises or the 'message(s)' it gives. These issues and messages need highlighting and scrutinising. But they are in part communicated by the form in which the film is experienced. We experience the film in itself *as* a challenge to mere rationality. Theology can thus in turn be challenged to think of how it, as a discipline, functions through more than mere rationality.

Sentimentality, I suggest, is more positive and significant in film and theology than film critics and theologians often allow. To characterise *Titanic* as a 'woman's film' obscures this insight for both women and men. The fact that the film does indeed have 'crossover appeal' shows that labelling it a woman's film misleads. It may be more appropriate to call it a historical epic, but containing all the flaws that are likely in a sentimental melodrama. As noted, huge numbers of women have enjoyed the film. Many watch it many times. More women than men attend churches in the West. It is not, however, immediately apparent that theology in Western churches, for so long dominated by male formulators, has adequately addressed emotional elements within it. Responses to a film such as *Titanic* perhaps suggest that appropriate reflection upon the place of emotion in Western culture would have both theological and broader cultural consequences for both women and men.

Mass Aestheticisation

Before I seek to draw together a number of theological threads which have run through this chapter, I turn to one further aspect of

---

[42] It is striking that the two main texts on theology and film in German known to me (I. Kirsner, *Erlösung im Film: Praktisch-theologische Analysen und Interpretation* and Herrmann, *Sinnmaschine Kino*) both appear in series of books of practical theology. Ulrike Vollmer has drawn my attention to other material from a German context, though acknowledged that most of the dialogue began in practical theology and largely remains there.

Titanic which invites critical reflection. In his consideration of the film, Jörg Herrmann draws attention to an 'enormous aestheticisation' (*'eine massive Ästhetisierung'*) of the catastrophic element in the film, which occurs in the portrayal of the circumstances surrounding the actual sinking of the ship.[43] The viewer is rendered safe and secure, Herrmann suggests, by the way that Cameron turns the horror of the sinking into a scene of beauty. Though this could be regarded as simply a further example of the sentimentalising (in the sense of simplifying) of the horror of the event, in this case I think more is at work.

It is necessary to ask why the sheer horror of the human tragedy is tamed in any way by the film. As Lubin points out, one of the film's main aims is to demonstrate the scale and emotional enormity of the human tragedy.[44] It achieves this particularly effectively because of the two levels of its story (past and present), whereby we, as viewers, also participate in the discoveries made by the technical crew on the salvage vessel, as we and they listen to Rose's story.[45] Lewis Bodine is the 'film's personification of modern emotional anaesthesia'[46] and may be more insensitive than many of the film's viewers, but this is precisely in order to shake the viewer out of any tendency in this direction.

Martin Barker's study of the film is also helpful here. Barker shows how a range of devices in the film bring about our identification with the salvage team. He shows how special effects, which hide themselves in the film, are used as 'emotional intensifications of the narrative meaning'. As Barker notes:

> At the start of the film, they [the salvage crew] are cynical money-grabbers, playing at understanding the scale of the tragedy but really in it for the potential wealth. But now they are faced with a truth larger than they had realised. Here was human hope and tragedy on a grand scale. Nothing directly signals such a change, but because of what we as audience have been shown – and see them as having seen – the film surely asks us to ask such a change of them. And it is precisely the special effects, acting as narrative intensifiers, which generate this requirement of us.[47]

---

[43] Herrmann, *Sinnmaschine Kino*, 203.
[44] Lubin, *Titanic*, 19–20. The charge of aestheticisation of human tragedy is also made of other films, e.g. by Schmucler of *Schindler's List*. See H. Schmucler, 'The scandal of aestheticising horror: thoughts on *Schindler's List'*, in *Media Development*).
[45] Brock Lovett especially, who is the character who finally 'gets' the human dimension of it all in a way he never has before. See Lubin, *Titanic*, 24.
[46] Lubin, *Titanic*, 19.
[47] Barker, *From Antz to Titanic*, 103.

In other words, the film is clever in its use of the illusory art of film making, in involving the viewer in the narrative (through the eyes of the salvage team) to get 'the point' that the salvage team itself eventually 'gets'. To use (old) Rose's words to Lewis Bodine 'Thank you for that fine forensic analysis, Mr Bodine. Of course the experience of it was somewhat different.'

All this being so, we must return to Herrmann's concern. If a main point of the film is to accentuate the human tragedy of the ship's sinking, and if this discovery is enabled via techniques used in the making of the film, why then the aestheticisation? Is this a disturbing form of 'beauty' such as prompted Damien Hirst to describe the flying of the planes into the Twin Towers as 'art' (a statement for which he later apologised)? We need to be clear: despite the seemingly graphic portrayal of the sinking, the horror is still sanitised. The lights remained burning on the ship in the film for longer than would have been possible. The film score covers the screams and hides the silences.

I suggest that this aspect of the film in fact runs counter to the positive aspect of its sentimentalising. Even though the film functions so well because of the way it works emotionally, when it comes to aesthetics, sentimentality has a less than positive effect. The clarification of the scale of the human tragedy worked well so long as there was congruence between the film's impact and its ideological thrust. Emotionally, a main point is for the viewer to *feel* that human reason is limited, both through experiencing Rose's story and through anger at those who build a ship claimed to be unsinkable and who push it to (and beyond) its limits. Suddenly, however, at the point of the ship's sinking, what we *see* becomes incongruous with what we are to *feel*. The full emotional impact is being softened. It is as if someone else is making the decision for us that we as viewers cannot bear too much reality.

What might account for this? I suggest that it is an example of what may be called the aestheticisation of death. At a time of widespread religious decline in the West, the ways in which people treat death and prepare for it are becoming diverse and fragmented. The arts are often themselves called the new religion. This means that, where discussion of death is not simply avoided altogether, there has been a shift in the institutional and cultural forms in which people deal with the prospect of death. Cinema-goers would expect to have to confront death in some way simply by going to the film of *Titanic*. But despite wanting to address the issue of the human scale of the tragedy, a film portrayal of death's full horror would certainly not have made too enjoyable an evening's viewing. In some ways, what the film has done, on the level of entertainment, is quite understandable. I suggest, however, that this avoidance strategy is more culturally-conditioned than first meets the eye. The awesome beauty of the portrayals of the sinking ship, and the resulting aftermath, represent the aesthetic response to the reality of death. It is the kind of response one would expect in a late-, or post-, modern culture.

Concluding Reflections

I began this chapter by suggesting the inevitability of looking at a film that has broken all records. Some account needed to be given of a film that most people have watched. Whether the film's success indicated mass escapism from more serious issues, that its viewers succumbed to skilful marketing or even simply that celebrities really do pull in big crowds, to fail to consider the film might have amounted to theology's proverbial avoidance of the popular. As it has turned out, I have suggested that discussion of the film and its reception are fruitful in many ways.

I proceeded on a directly theological note by juxtaposing two film critics' responses to the film, using the work of David Lubin to test out the accuracy of the insights offered on the film by Ryan Gilbey. I suggested that Ryan Gilbey's critique of the film merely highlights a cultural deficiency: we do not really know how to handle theological questions adequately in public any more. Gilbey's critique highlights the fact that contemporary God-talk within art criticism and popular culture can constrain creative theology and limit the possibility of theological and religious insight contributing to society's self-criticism and to cultural development.

Turning to the question of genre, I noted the way in which the categorisation of *Titanic* has also limited its potential impact. Of particular concern were assumed definitions of what constitutes the sentimental and sentimentality in film. This will prove a crucial component in my overall thesis in this present book.

Finally, I expressed concern at the film's handling of death. Rather than locate such a critique within a general rejection either of such a film or of entertainment in general, I sought to show that the film remains theologically helpful in so far as it presents an example of how contemporary Western culture is dealing with death. In making such an observation it would be wrong to suggest that religions and theology are automatically detached from such cultural considerations in their own contemporary dealing with death. On the contrary, the immersion of all theology within culture merely accentuates the need for theological reflection itself to be culturally astute, whilst playing its role of offering both culturally apposite interpretations of reality, and, where appropriate, critical responses to features of culture which stifle human flourishing.

Case-Study C

Film Genres and the Habit of Cinema-Going

One way in which film-watching patterns can be shaped is by viewing particular types of film. There are fans of horror films, science fiction, disaster movies, romantic comedies, westerns, action movies, thrillers, period dramas, erotic films, historical dramas, and war movies. Each of these genres offers to a viewer in a standard format a sustained engagement with a particular range of themes. Films within a particular genre work by satisfying a viewer's expectations, whilst seeking to offer a novel enough plot and convincing enough characters to maintain fresh interest. I go to a horror film in order to be scared, though within a safe environment. I watch a period drama to become lost in the history and culture of the period in question. I watch a romantic comedy in order to laugh and to weep. In each of these cases, if my expectations are not satisfied then I am likely to be disappointed by the film. Locating a film within a genre is an important aspect in film-making, and above all in film-marketing and distribution.[1]

For the purposes of this present book, the influence of film-watching according to genre upon the shaping of a viewer's experience is highly significant. Some form of emotional impact of film remains constant across the genres. What differ are the particular emotions aroused and their intensity.[2] Fear may be experienced in horror, in thrillers or war films. Sadness and happiness may mingle in different proportions in 'weepies' and romantic comedies. Anger may be kindled in certain types of thriller, or in historical dramas, where injustices are portrayed. As important as emotional responses are, however, watching films within genres proves

---

[1] Turner, *Film as Social Practice*, 97–101

[2] Though intensity cannot, of course, be easily predicted, either in relation to genres or specific films as it relates as much to what particular viewers bring to films. I mean simply that one might expect a more intense emotional experience through watching a psychological thriller than a family comedy.

significant also due to the regular exposure which viewers experience to particular questions and issues. Cinema-goers who are regular watchers of thrillers expect to be confronted not simply with a battle of good and evil, but with uncertainty, unpredictability and ambiguity. The shock element within the genre guarantees unexpected plot twists and fosters mistrust of leading characters. The thought that human beings really are very complex is consistently reinforced for a person who is a regular watcher of thrillers.

There is a parallel with the world of theology here. In its cognitive aspect, Christian theology requires people constantly to engage with a range of themes. God (as Trinity), Jesus Christ, Holy Spirit, creation, salvation, human being, church, ministry and sacraments are standard headings addressed in theology textbooks. A feature of theological discussion is which of these themes, if any, controls the others, or on which more emphasis should be placed. But to leave any one of them out of the picture altogether would be seriously to distort a theology. It is, then, as wrong to neglect one as it is to over-emphasise any one at the expense of others. Each needs the other to form a coherent whole.

The range of film genres does not function in exactly the same way, but there are similarities. It is simply not true that you have to like all genres. Personality type and life experience may influence a person not to like a particular genre of film. A person haunted by a war experience may not be able, for example, to watch a war movie. There is, however, a similarity between the range of genres and the themes of theology insofar as the restriction of the film-watching experience is likely to distort a person's perception of human experience. Science fiction films are always also 'about' contemporary human experience even whilst provoking the imagination. They may not, however, be able adequately to cover all the emotions and life-issues which the habit of watching a range of genres would address. Horror films rarely only have the purpose of taking a viewer through a range of types of fear. The ones that work best (*The Shining* is a prime example) also have a good storyline to enable the fear experience to be connected with apparent normality. But they are not likely to tap the viewer's experience of loving relationships and family life in quite the same way as, say, a romantic comedy. Attention to film genre as an aspect of the habit of film-watching is therefore, like attention to the range of themes with which Christian theology is required to deal, two-edged. In keeping with the theoretical line emerging throughout this book I want in this short case study to refer to romantic comedies as an example of both the strength and limitation of 'keeping with a genre' when watching films.

Romantic comedies are perhaps the quintessential form of feel-good movie for adults. Often also functioning as films which arouse emotions and raise questions about family life, they usually turn out happily, endeavour to make the viewer feel warm and affirmed, and connect with whatever loving relationships a viewer currently enjoys.[3] They are positive, life-affirming films which usually play down the negative aspects of ordinary life, brush over life's complexities in their desire to show that life really is largely about dating and mating, though also therefore about 'love, actually'. The charge of escapism is thus sure to be levelled at the cinema-goer who enjoys a regular diet of romantic comedies. Watching *When Harry Met Sally*, *Sleepless in Seattle* and *You've Got Mail*, or *Four Weddings and a Funeral*, *Notting Hill* and *Love Actually* will produce a very different view of life from frequent encounter with the films of Ken Loach and Mike Leigh, for example.

In a report of a 2000 lecture given by the then Archbishop of Wales (now Archbishop of Canterbury) – 'Trite films fail to show true love, says bishop' – Rowan Williams is quoted as criticising the portrayal of relationships in *Notting Hill*. Challenging the implication that the 'clumsy courtship' between Anna Scott (Julia Roberts) and William Thacker (Hugh Grant) should be held up as a romantic ideal, Williams commends as 'far more erotic' the relationship between Max (Tim McInnerny) and Bella (Gina McKee). The latter is paralysed and unable to have children, yet 'every word and gesture they come out with is full of absolute mutual joy'.

Williams is surely right in his judgment. The scene where Max carries Bella up the stairs of their house, an ordinary daily ritual, is a powerful expression of both the nature and practical outworking of their love for each other. It is not a customary feature of romantic comedy. But this is also, I think, a point at which screenplay-writer Richard Curtis shows he has managed to subvert elements of the

---

[3] Three qualifications are needed here. A romantic comedy may not always end happily. *Shirley Valentine*, for example, ends ambiguously. The ending may, however, indicate that it slips out of the genre and becomes more clearly a 'women's film'. Second, whatever a film endeavours to do may not always work. A romantic comedy does not intend to make a person unhappy but may do so if a person seeks a loving relationship and cannot find one. Leaving the cinema can therefore be a sad experience due to the return to 'real life'. The film-watching may have been escapist but valuable nevertheless. Third, despite the fact that '... *Chasing Amy* ... and *As Good as it Gets* ... have expanded the genre's traditional focus on the heterosexual couple' (Blandford et al. *Film Studies Directory*, 202), it must be acknowledged that the genre operates almost exclusively with respect to heterosexual relationships.

comedy/romantic comedy genre. Whilst maintaining the feel-good factor which is central to such films, he has also shifted from the sentimental to the poignant in each of the three comedies he has written. And, as this book is making clear, I am hesitant about the 'sentimental' being too easily used as a negative term anyway. Romantic comedies are too easily labelled 'trite'. When interpreted and explored in the context of their function, there is much more to them than first meets the eye.[4] Williams' criticism is thus in danger of paying too little attention to the complexity of the practice of film-watching, with regard to watching a whole film, to respecting a film's overall emotional response, and to acknowledging that a film is often reflected on in the company of others. Furthermore, it gives little credit to the intelligence of film-audiences.

I wish to suggest a simple but crucially important function for the regular watching of romantic comedies: they focus on the centrality for human life of loving relationships. Whatever the strengths and limitations of any particular films, so long as there are some high quality films amongst a batch watched – and *Four Weddings and a Funeral*, *Notting Hill* and *Love Actually* are certainly that[5] – then the stimulus for enjoyment of and reflection upon loving relationships pushes well beyond 'feel-good escapism'. To conclude that regular watching of romantic comedies is inevitably distorting of real human relationships is as crass an oversimplification as saying at the opposite pole that those who attend Christian worship, and say a prayer of confession on a regular basis, become depressed individuals. The latter can happen. But both such oversimple judgments overlook the broader context (social and psychological) within which each activity occurs.

Romantic comedies are, in fact, a challenge to 'feel-bad religion'. To respect the way in which this happens, however, requires a broad understanding of how feel-good movies work, and a recognition that religion does not, on the whole, make people feel bad. There is bad religion about. But good religion knows what to do with romantic comedies. Rather than religion and romantic

---

[4] In Williams' defence, the report in *The Times* nowhere signals that Williams himself used the term 'trite' of the film. In fact, he commended watching of the film in marriage preparation *because of* Max and Bella's relationship!

[5] Of the three, *Love Actually* has received the most negative response from film-critics. Again, though, the same mix of sentiment and poignancy is evident. Film-watchers largely seem to disagree with the film's negative critics, and apparently receive more from the film than a mere feel-good sensation through their interaction with it.

comedies being viewed (negatively) under a banner of 'sentimental-ity', I suggest that enjoyment and critical reception of each can be recognised as cultural ways for shaping experience and approach-ing the future positively.

Good religion in a Christian form knows, however, that there is a critical voice that must be raised against a sole diet of romantic comedies. A film-watching habit which meant a person watched little else might render a person incapable of registering negative aspects of life. The significance of the tough parts of the Curtis films, for example, would be overlooked. In theological terms, this would be like trying to live life as a constant reflection of resurrec-tion without death (which would then be no resurrection at all). This simple case study of romantic comedies therefore serves as a reminder that a film-watching habit too tightly focused on a single genre may prove unhelpful in terms of film's contribution to per-sonal development. Admittedly, the viewing patterns of an individ-ual viewer are rarely so clear-cut.[6] It may be that without some sort of reflective process being encouraged, regular cinema-goers are less clear about their watching patterns or the impact of particular genres upon them. But more research is clearly needed here.

---

[6] Save perhaps for an obsessive fan of a genre. Such a state of affairs may, however, have little to do with films and film-watching per se.

5

The Reception of Film in Theological Perspective

Illusion

One of the most widely-quoted chapters from *Explorations in Theology and Film* is David Jasper's critical response to the whole enterprise. One of Jasper's main points was that theology 'whether within the Judaeo-Christian tradition or otherwise, emerges from more problematic and disturbing material than Hollywood dare show'. Recognising that the cinema 'is, by its very nature, a house of illusions', and also that theology 'needs its own illusions in order to do its work', he stressed, nevertheless, that we must 'be perpetually watchful that the illusions of the screen do not also include the illusion of theology in a mere celluloid simulacrum of redemption and salvation'.[1] To change the image, Jasper is suggesting that there is a great danger, when theology is easily found 'in', or in response to film, that salvation is found on the cheap. Chris Arthur is similarly cautious:

> ... there is a sense [in *Explorations in Theology and Film*] of sleeping theological watchdogs, overcome by films' enticing narcotic mix of popularity, relevance, excitement, pleasure, interest, and wrestling in their dreams with seemingly wonderful "resource material" as, almost unremarked upon, a theft – spiritual, intellectual, moral – of almost incalculable scale is being perpetrated.[2]

Both are surely right with their warnings. But both critiques are themselves too simple. There is a disturbing suspicion of the popular here. There is also an easy ascription of illusion to film,

[1] Jasper, 'On Systematizing the Unsystematic', 244 (cf. also 240); cited, e.g. in Deacy, *Screen Christologies*, 9, 105; Coates, *Romantic Legacy*.
[2] C. Arthur, 'Review of "Explorations in Theology and Film"', in *Media Development* 2 (1998), 60.

without religion's own use of illusion being equally critiqued. In this section I explore how important illusions are in human self-understanding, in a way which brings theology and film closer together than may be first thought.

The cinema is a house of illusions. It is a place where a highly complex technical exercise bears fruit in the form of an entertaining sound and light show. By entering into a cinema, viewers collude with the illusion, for example, that they are seeing a ship sink, a building explode, witnessing a relationship break down. Most directors are keen to maximise the sense of illusion, to make it easier for viewers to collude. But it is clear to all parties what is going on. Popular films (as opposed to art films) are not only illusions; they are highly simplified, often formulaic illusions.[3] But even Jasper recognises that theology works with illusions too.

The exploration of how films work *as* 'illusions' should be the prompt for one of the main, fruitful results of the theology/religion-film dialogue.

An illusion is not a delusion.[4] Standard dictionaries tend to hide this important distinction, suggesting that the two terms are synonymous. If an illusion is a 'discrepancy from truth' – visual or otherwise – it need not carry connotations of active deception. In terms of sight, an illusion is something which appears to be there. It is not really there, but there is nevertheless something in need of reception and interpretation. Illusions command a viewer's attention. Speaking of visual illusions, Gregory writes: 'Illusions are "subjective" in our experience, and they affect behaviour and skill'.[5] Illusions thus require us to sharpen our vision (literally and metaphorically), both in the contexts in which they appear, and more generally. They may be called 'true lies' in so far as they may make no attempt to present 'things as they really are', but nevertheless draw out of the viewer a concern for what is true. In the case of graphic illusions (e.g. the drawings of Maurits Escher), 'what really is' is in theory 'plain to see', on a page. But the interplay between image and viewer complicates the process of clarifying what 'really is'. Visual illusions thus function as a good example of what has long been explored in the world of texts and literary interpretation, and increasingly so in recent decades: the role of the reader/receiver/interpreter in the task of interpretation.

---

[3] Herrmann, *Sinnmaschine Kino*, 88–93.
[4] This point, important for Freud (who thought, however, that the illusions of religion are also delusions) is picked up, of example, in G. Loughlin, *Alien Sex: The Body and Desire in Cinema and Theology*, 55–6.
[5] R.L. Gregory (ed.), *The Oxford Companion to the Mind*, 337.

By contrast, a delusion is a 'fixed, idiosyncratic belief, unusual in the culture to which the person belongs'.[6] In this light, though in common speech we may call a person 'deluded' for having an erroneous idea, the use of such a heavy, technical term for simply being misguided or mistaken is fraught with difficulty. Discussing the worlds of religion and film-watching in relation to this important distinction between illusion and delusion, then, becomes crucial. For it can be readily accepted that both religion and film depend on illusions.[7] Only religion's critics, and only film's critics (and film critics!) hostile to the level of immersion of the viewer in the film-watching experience or the oversimplifications of plot and characterisation to which popular films are prone, equate illusion with delusion. The recognition of a necessary detachment from the experience of immersion in an illusory world is, however, part of the experience of being religious and being a committed film-watcher. Christians know that bread and wine remain bread and wine, even whilst disagreeing amongst themselves about how to speak of the presence of Christ in relation to these elements of the Communion service. It is not delusory to view these symbols sacramentally: the interaction between them and those who consume them can do something to the people who partake.

An experience of religious commitment of this type and an experience of watching a film can sharpen perception. Such sharpening of perception works on at least two levels: literal and figurative. Attentive film-watching can help with physical perception: you watch more closely, even when you know you are being deceived (e.g. by special effects). Religious believers who use visual images in their spiritual lives can also be better trained, noticing more in icons and paintings, for example.

'Perception' works figuratively too. Deeper 'seeing' may not, however, simply be the preserve of the religious. Film-watching at its best not only trains sight. It makes use of sight and emotional involvement to make a person more critical of what they see and experience. In this respect, watching a film is not simply 'like' attending a service of worship (it's just that the former sharpens your capacity for 'seeing' how films work, and the latter attends to something which may be called 'spiritual perception'). The analogues at work are more complex, entailing visual, emotional, moral and cognitive 'ways of seeing', present in *both* experiences, even if sometimes in radically different ways.

---

[6] Gregory (ed.), *Oxford Companion to the Mind*, 184.
[7] It is, though, fair to say that much religion operates with what be termed 'verbal illusions', such as myth, legend, metaphor, and symbolic language.

'Illusion' is not to be opposed to 'reality' in any simple sense. Even Freud's definition of 'illusion' may be regarded as closer to 'myth' than 'delusion' or 'unreality'.[8] Once this is acknowledged, then the importance of the cognitive worlds within which the processing of human experiences occurs is recognised too. Cognitive psychology corrects the psychological reductionism resulting from many psychoanalytic accounts of human experience (and of the film-watching experience[9]) but retains interest in the multiple aspects of the hermeneutical task. When Watts comments that the 'concerns of cognitive psychology here seem to be somewhat broader than those of hermeneutics',[10] his definition of 'hermeneutics' is perhaps too narrow. He is working within too constrained a model of literary hermeneutics. However, his point that interpretation (of human experience, of any work of art) is a multi-dimensional matter remains valid. When he goes on to comment that 'religion, art and play perhaps have it in common that they are imaginative, and equip people for conduct in the real world, even though they are not content with descriptions of the obvious features of that world', he is surely correct. The use of cognitive psychology in film reception thus discloses the way in which emotion and cognition interweave in the experience of interpretation of any work of art. The illusions of film are functionally no different from the truthful fiction of a thoughtful novelist. They may merely be fictions in visual form. Human beings need such fictions and such illusions in order playfully to reflect on life.

'Illusion', then, must not be seen in negative terms. In terms of film-watching experience, illusions are precisely what are enjoyed and 'used' by the film-watcher. To suggest such illusions are more dangerous than many interpreters acknowledge, as Jasper comes close to doing, is to miss one of the main points of cinema. Or to imply that religious meanings are somehow always inevitably more transparent and morally truthful than what one sees on screen seems overly optimistic. That Jasper's criticisms are launched especially at Hollywood films may be understandable. But even here, caution is needed. His critique may come close to prioritising art films over popular films, as if the latter are especially more illusory (and thus distorting and dangerous). To his great credit, however, he does acknowledge that: 'Where ... the cinema comes closest to stimulating theological reflection ... is not by its themes or specific

[8] F. Watts, *Theology and Psychology*, 154.
[9] C. Plantinga and G.M. Smith (eds.), *Passionate Views: Film, Cognition, and Emotion*, 10–13; Barker, *From Antz to Titanic*, 13–15.
[10] Watts, *Theology and Psychology*, 154.

motifs ... but by its very form and nature'.[11] In what follows, I hope to show how true this is, but that Jasper's insight pertains also to those films about which he is so critical.

Religions make claims to be far from illusion in the sense that they deal with what 'really is' in and beyond death as well as in life. But they do so with reference to a wide range of stories and rituals. It is true that 'more problematic and disturbing material than Hollywood dare show' gives rise to theology. It is also true that events of global significance – such as 9/11, the ensuing 'war against terrorism' and the many terrorist attacks on West-related targets around the world – disclose the complex way in which religion and violence interweave. From the perspective of any religious tradition it would be clear that 'doing away with religion' would not solve this. The mysteries of a humanity which always seems able to work simultaneously for good and ill are difficult to fathom. But there are no illusions here. Religions and the cinema are, however, in the same business as far as their practices are concerned in relation to such clearly non-illusory events. They provide locations and rituals in and through which participants in their practices can clarify what is and is not illusory. They have other functions, too, which make them diverge (religions have a social function, the cinema entertains). But their ritual focus is on the evocation of an experience which moves, provokes and gets people thinking. If the ways in which they offer these practices differ, this is because of the broader cognitive worlds in which *as practices* they are located. Oversimplified polarities between church and cinema will not work. Nor must the potential of either practice (churchgoing or film-watching) to be informative and transformatory be read as located solely either in the practice itself ('the service' or 'the film') or the participant ('the churchgoer' or 'the viewer').

Emotion

The second important heading in this distillation of how the film-theology/religion dialogue works is 'emotion'. Films work in large part through playing on viewers' emotions. This was crystal clear in relation to the two films to which I have devoted most space in this book. Films are not, of course, exclusively visual vehicles for emotional stimulation. They stimulate the senses in visual and aural ways. But any study of film-watching which did not account for their emotional impact would have to be regarded as deficient. In this present book, however, I wish to argue that it is precisely at this

---

[11] Jasper, 'On Systematizing the Unsystematic', 240.

point that the contemporary dialogue between theology/religion and film/film studies needs to be developed. Unlike Steve Nolan, however, I am far from convinced that the best way of conducting such an enquiry is with respect to psychoanalytic film theory, especially since such film theory is itself under severe challenge from within the world of film studies.[12] My argument is this: there is widespread evidence that film-watching can 'do something' to people emotionally. It is difficult to theorise adequately, especially since different films do different things to people, but the theorising is nevertheless worth engaging in. It is even more difficult to assess what lasting influence and ideological or behavioural change, if any, may result from the emotional impact of films. As many interpreters acknowledge, however, much more empirical research in this field is needed before firm conclusions can be drawn.[13]

The emotional response of viewers is a key component in how films also come to function cognitively. Cognitive psychology supplies a theoretical framework within which the power of films can be understood. People may go to the cinema for 'sheer entertainment'. But the extent to which they are 'moved' by films may entail more than a mere damp eye at the cinema, and have consequences well beyond the cinema-visit itself. How, though, does this enormous emotional impact of film come about? Whole books are written on the topic.[14] Here I can only be selective, and run the risk of highlighting evidence conducive to my argument. But at least such evidence exists.

I have already drawn extensively on Tan and Frijda's work, and will do so again in the next section. Here I cite two further examples of how emotions play a crucial part in the film-watching experience in a way which interweaves with a theological reception of film. The first comes from Eitzen's study of the emotional basis of film comedy. He suggests:

---

[12] S. Nolan, 'Towards a New Religious Film Criticism: Using Film to Understand Religious Identity Rather than Locate Cinematic Analogue', in J. Mitchell and S. Marriage (eds.), *Meditating Religion: Conversations in Media, Religion and Culture* (London and New York: Continuum, 2003), 169–78. I shall pick up this conversation again in Chapter 6 when reviewing the possible ways of drawing on contemporary film-theology/religion debates.

[13] Barker, *From Antz to Titanic*; Lyden 2003. Davies and Pearson 2003 provides a good example of how such research might be conducted. As this book goes to press, research funded by the Methodist Church in Great Britain is being conducted in this area by Charlotte Haines Lyen.

[14] E.g. E.S. Tan, *Emotion and the Structure of Narrative Film: Film as an Emotion Machine*; T. Grodal, *Pictures: A New Theory of Film Genres, Feelings and Cognition*; Plantinga and Smith (eds.), *Passionate Views.*

What the average moviegoer wants most of all from movies is not narrative per se but strong and concentrated affective responses. *Movies can provide a powerful emotional kick in a safe context.* This is what mainstream audiences have always been most eager to pay for in movies – not just the pleasure of seeing a problem through, but the concentrated experience of emotions that are not often triggered in day-to-day affairs: sadness, horror, fear, excitement, the happiness associated with the climax of a romance, the thrill of having survived a brush with death, and ... the funny side of inappropriate behavior.[15]

This is a striking description of the film-watching experience. It implies more than a hint of escapism. But we may call it an 'empowering escapism'. The 'concentrated experience of emotions' compensates for what is lacking in the rest of the structure of a viewer's life. Experiencing such concentrated emotions via the cinema enables a viewer to live life more fully. The rest of life becomes more bearable because of the cinematic experience. The film is in this sense, then, an empowering medium.

Striking, too, in this suggestion by Eitzen, of course, is that so much of what is described could apply to Christian worship, when the *function* of worship is considered. It is surely far from coincidental that one of the two forms of worship which are numerically strongest at the present – the evangelical – certainly provides 'a powerful emotional kick'.[16] Granted that all forms of worship are in some sense escapist, the main question is what the escapism is about and for. Here, I suggest, in the midst of discussing film-watching as a fundamentally emotional experience, we find a satisfactory answer. The emotional arousal will be unhealthily escapist when not integrated within a cognitive framework capable of grasping a person's life-structure. In other words, if a viewer him- or herself fails to see how this 'powerful emotional kick' is located within their life as a whole, then it may contribute to the negative sense of films' 'illusory' character to which Jasper drew attention.

---

[15] Eitzen, 'Emotional Basis', 91; my emphasis.
[16] The other form of worship attracting new support is highly formal liturgical worship (e.g. Anglo-/Roman Catholic or Orthodox). It would be too simple to suggest that the evangelical and liturgical forms simply appeal to emotional and aesthetic emphases in worship (and to corresponding personality types of worshippers). For one thing, evangelical worship is not without aesthetic considerations and is often liturgical; for another formal, liturgical worship moves people. More significantly, I think, lurks a tendency, even in theological engagement with such issues, to relate emotion with 'kitsch' and aesthetics to 'art'. This is deeply damaging of both styles of worship (and the theological emphases related to them).

The point at issue here, though, is that we are dealing here with an *emotional* response to a film. A viewer may watch a film for this emotional experience, not primarily for education or cognitive stimulus. The fact that emotional responses are themselves located within a wider cognitive framework (by which human beings process the different aspects of their experience) is, however, crucial. We see, therefore, the potential of film-watching as a practice to be a crucially integrative human practice in Western culture. In the habits which surround a cinema-going experience (friendships, eating with others, journeying to and from a multiplex, sexual encounter), a person may find the various aspects of their life being structured, in response to the trigger provided by a fundamental arousal of a range of human emotions in the film-watching experience itself.

A second example of the centrality of emotion in the film-watching experience is provided by Berys Gaut. As Gaut notes, it is 'part of the folk wisdom of responding to films (and to literature) that audiences sometimes identify with characters, that the success or failure of a film partly depends on whether this identification occurs, and that the quality and strength of emotional responses depend on identification'.[17] Gaut then subjects this folk wisdom to critical scrutiny. He concludes that identification undoubtedly does occur, but that in order to understand how, one needs to respect what he calls 'aspectual identification'.[18] Viewers do not (cannot, usually) identify with characters in all respects. What happens is that in a variety of ways viewers end up empathising, and sometimes sympathising, with characters. Sometimes this is a result of film technique (particular camera angles which require us to take up particular viewpoints); at other times it may result from what the viewer him- or herself brings to the film. Identification, we may say, may thus end up with an emotional emphasis, but not always begin in the affective realm.

Where the emotional aspect of identification leads to becomes of particular interest. Here, Gaut's conclusion – borne out in relation to two examples, *The Crying Game* and *Letter from an Unknown Woman* – is striking. He writes: 'Identification, then, plays an important role in our emotional responses to films. It also plays a significant part in teaching us how to respond emotionally to fictionally delineated situations'.[19] The process of identification

---

[17] B. Gaut, 'Identification and Emotion in Narrative Film', in C. Plantinga and G.M. Smith (eds.), *Passionate Views: Film, Cognition and Emotion*, 200.

[18] Gaut, 'Identification and Emotion', 206.

[19] Gaut, 'Identification and Emotion', 213.

which can occur in film-watching, then, can function educationally, regardless of whether film carries a didactic purpose as such. Film-watching enables viewers to grow and develop as people, in their emotional literacy and, as Gaut goes on to show, in their moral development as a result of working with their emotional responses. In drawing on responses to *The Crying Game*, he concludes: 'Here identification with a character whose attitudes towards homosexuality change fundamentally in the course of the film also encourages the audience through empathy to want the [homosexual] relationship to work out, and thus also encourages them to question their attitudes toward homosexuality.'[20]

Identification with the lead characters was, of course, a crucial part of the success of *Titanic*, especially in the case of young women's identification with Rose.[21] The film also serves, however, as an example of the limitations of emotional identification in film when characterisation is thin. Though the experience of watching *Titanic* undoubtedly supplies 'a powerful emotional kick' for all viewers, Rose is arguably the only character capable of supporting any sustained emotional attachment for viewers. Even Jack, in his heroism, is undeveloped. Cal is a 'cardboard villain'[22], as is the iron-ically-named Lovejoy. And the 'teen-romance ideology' within which the film is played out[23] constrains the potential range of emotional identification which viewers may enjoy and therefore any development they may experience. But far from altering the accuracy of the perception that the emotional impact of a film is a key, if not the primary, means through which a viewer responds to the 'film experience' this merely confirms it. The film works at an emotional level, but it works more for women viewers simply because there is only one character with whom viewers have a chance to empathise.[24] The limited options of identification indicate a weakness of the film, despite its extraordinary success.

The process of identification with characters serves, then, as a reminder of how all narrative art can work. The same effect can result from reading biblical narratives. That this is so explains why narrative theology has made a huge contribution to fresh exploration of biblical texts. The potential of biblical texts is being recognised not only by those who approach them with a theological

---

[20] Gaut, 'Identification and Emotion', 214.
[21] Lubin, *Titanic*, 11–12.
[22] Lubin, *Titanic*, 96.
[23] Lubin, *Titanic*, 65.
[24] And it must be accepted that identification may not be possible for all women viewers.

interest. Biblical narratives are accessible because of their proven capacity to work as texts embodying characters with whom reader and hearers can readily identify.

The rediscovery of biblical narratives in this way, and the possibility of readers identifying with characters has, however, also led to extensive use of biblical role-play in ways that do not always enlighten. Invitations to 'feel your way into the characters' may not even approximate to the extent to which the illusions created by the world of film lure viewers into identification with film characters. As any readers who have experience here will know, successful Bible study, which knows how to use literary methods of reading (and to handle groups in the task of exploring characters through emotional identification) is one thing. Badly-led Bible studies which encourage mere self-expression, the cost of attentiveness to a biblical text are quite another.

Films present to the viewer via a carefully-crafted multi-sensual medium a range of characters that one is invited to evaluate and with whom one may empathise. We will be manipulated, for sure. Will our emotional responses be wholly controlled? No; they cannot be, however much manipulation may go on. The extent to which a viewer may or may not detach him- or herself from emotional immersion in the experience of watching will, however, be dependent on many other factors yet to be explored.

A final feature of the emotional dimension of film-watching which should be noted, and which makes cinema very close to religious community, is the concept of a 'safe context'. It was there in Eitzen's summary description of what viewers can gain from the film-watching experience. It is echoed in many other ways in analyses of film-watching (e.g. especially in studies of horror movies). A frequently explored issue here is whether the emotions felt when watching a film are 'real emotions'. For this would affect what is then 'done' with the emotions roused in, for example, a reflective process beyond the watching of a film. The emotions roused by a disaster movie cannot be the same as those experienced by people really inside a burning tower block (*The Towering Inferno*), for example, or in an upturned ship (*The Poseidon Adventure*). Nor can the experience of watching a horror or crime thriller be the same as actually being pursued by a serial killer. But though these particular examples are surely accurate, matters are not always so simple. Few viewers of *The Shawshank Redemption* will identify with Red because of their own experience as murderers. Gaut's insight into 'aspectual identification' is again relevant. The real emotion that viewers do bring to this film is the sense of guilt or remorse that they feel about a past action of their own. The awareness that a cinema provides a 'safe context' for such an experience is of utmost importance, especially because emotional responses cannot always be controlled.[25] In this connection between emotional arousal, the potential for emotional development/learning through the film-watching experience and the concept of a 'safe context', the potential parallels with participation in a religious community become very apparent once more.[26]

The notion of a religion/theology-film dialogue focussing on the emotional impact of film-watching will be greeted with the gravest suspicion by many contemporary theologians. It may (just) be deemed acceptable to try to have a conversation with a film's themes. Whether or not a film 'has' an implicit theology, it might be considered acceptable to bring a theological framework to issues that a film raises. But to try to work theologically with a film in relation to the emotions it may arouse is another matter. This is tantamount to taking the subjective turn in theology to its logical, and alarming, conclusion. It is autobiographical theology at its worst.

Not surprisingly, I want to challenge such a view head-on. In the first place, attention to the emotional life is an important aspect of theological enquiry. In whatever form, then, the exposure of emotion is made possible in a safe environment; this should be of great interest to those keen to promote theological reflection. Second, to highlight the importance of attention to emotion is not the same as collapsing theology's subject matter into emotion or subjectivity. It will be crucial even in the context of this present work to clarify how exploration of emotion relates to other aspects of theology's task, but theology should welcome the stimulus which film-watching provides to address this aspect of human experience.

---

[25] Showing the film *Shirley Valentine* can evoke deep displays of emotion amongst middle-aged men and women. I have often been surprised at the rather snooty reactions shown to my interest in this film's impact on viewers. One cultural studies lecturer suggested to me it is 'pure froth'. One theology lecturer expressed disbelief that any theology could be explored in conversation with it (whilst an Anglican clergyman urged me to go much further than I did in C. Marsh, 'The Spirituality of *Shirley Valentine*' in C. Marsh and G. Ortiz (eds.), *Explorations in Theology and Film* in exploring Shirley Valentine's praying habits). It is a light comedy, a popular film with no pretensions to cinematic greatness. But what it achieves, especially in relation to its emotional impact, makes it worthy of close scrutiny. Its open ending subverts the genre in which it sits. Some simple dramatic devices make it an extremely interesting example of how a film can 'work'.

[26] Though it should be said that the notion of churches as 'safe spaces' has received major setbacks in recent years due to high-profile sex abuse cases.

Third, it is not only within worship, in charismatic or Pentecostal forms of theology, or in the cooler analysis of a pastoral theology seminar that emotions should be displayed and explored. Emotions are a part of human living and their exploration is thus a part of theological enquiry per se. If enjoyment of God, and clarification of who and what God is, is not to be confined only to the intellect and to rationality, then theological exploration must include more than mere passing reference to the emotional life.[27]

A key role that the theology/religion-film dialogue can play, therefore, begins at precisely the point where Barker concludes his 2000 study *From Antz to Titanic*. Noting that his pro-filmic methodology is 'a range of tools and techniques for approaching individual films, and the way they structure an audience's participative role',[28] he goes on to admit that when it comes to audiences' 'affective relations with films' he is less sure. He knows 'of few if any procedures for exploring how emotional responses to film might be structured'.[29] My contention is that theology is one important conversation partner in the task of structuring emotional responses by viewers to film. Theologies brought to film must resist the tendency to 'correct' films or their impact, or merely to impose a worldview upon a film or its watchers. But given that any theology worthy of the name will address human concerns at the deepest possible level, it cannot but be keen to respond to and dialogue with an art-form which at its best has the potential to expose human experience at its rawest. I stress that this is not simply about what is on screen, but about the results of the interplay between what is on screen, and the viewer. I also emphasise that the theological value of film-watching is not here being reduced to a matter of collecting 'emotional highs'. Gordon Lynch has recently begun to examine a range of contemporary experiences, especially amongst the young, which can be said to be providing meaning in life, which relate to intense experience, and which, for many, have replaced religion.[30] I am, however, keen to see explored the way in which film-watching, understood as an 'intensification of experience', provides an ordinary channel through which viewers are provoked to 'see' more deeply. In this section, I have suggested that it is clearly through emotional means that this intensification in the film-watching

---

[27] Admittedly, this acknowledgement runs the risk of reducing religion to its therapeutic aspect. To recognise that religion functions therapeutically need not, however, mean reducing it to that function.

[28] Barker, *From Antz to Titanic*, 193.

[29] Barker, *From Antz to Titanic*, 194.

[30] G. Lynch, *After Religion: 'Generation X' and the Search for Meaning*; cf. also Hughes, *Worship as Meaning*, 274–5.

experience occurs, and thus becomes part of theology's subject matter.

How this fundamental emotional arousal is adequately to form a starting point for theological reflection still needs much more unpacking, and would take us far beyond what it is possible for this book to achieve. I shall, however, address the point more directly below, and again in Chapter 6 when reviewing the ways in which the theology/religion-film dialogue has often been conducted.

Embodiment

Emotions are felt. They are experienced by people who have (indeed, are) bodies. A number of recent writers on theology and film draw attention to this aspect of film-watching.[31] For example, in exploring 'the Other' and 'otherness' as portrayed in and through monsters and aliens in popular culture, Elaine Graham critically examines 'the implicit metaphysical and theological values embedded' in such portrayals. She is concerned to probe what she calls the 'ontological hygiene' by which 'for the past three hundred years Western culture has drawn the fault-lines that separate humans, nature and machines'.[32] Human self-definition has, during this period, depended upon a quest for 'ontological purity', delineating the human in contrast to technology and the rest of the animal world and nature. Preoccupation with reason, empiricism and objectivity accompanied this quest,[33] though this entailed ultimately a lack of attention to diverse ways of being human, and also to differing ways of understanding embodiment.

In its attention to embodiment, Graham's study coheres well with this present enquiry. Her work serves as a reminder that attention to the emotional impact of film requires equal attention to the reception and exploration of such emotional responses as embodied responses. Recognition of the embodied form in which emotions are felt means that emotional responses are not reducible to psychological or physiological (let alone philosophical or theological) generalisations. Her critical analysis also serves as a reminder that attention to embodiment in theology can itself claim a history. Though it has a recent history,[34] it is also part of a 'Romantic

---

[31] Plate, 'Religion/Literature/Film', 28–9; E. Graham, *Representations of the post/human: Monsters, aliens and others in popular culture*; G. Ward, *True Religion*, Loughlin, *Alien Sex*.
[32] Graham, *Representations*, 11.
[33] Graham, *Representations*, 29.
[34] On which, see e.g. Loughlin, *Alien Sex*, xix–xx.

Legacy' which exists in a theological form.[35] Theology which fails
to address the intensity of embodied human experience would, in
this light, not be an adequate theology, because of its failure to
acknowledge the creatureliness of those articulating it.

Embodiment in the sense I am exploring here, however, is not
confined to its exploration as a theme *in* film. I want to explore the
notion of embodiment as an aspect of the film-watching experience.
Film-watching is frequently a visceral experience. Our guts often
feel something first when our emotions cause us to feel bodily
effects. Noel Carroll's work has proved important here. Carroll
explores in relation to the film-watching experience how emotions,
cognition and bodily experience inter-relate. Resisting the view that
emotions are simply bodily feeling – 'since sheer bodily feelings lack
intentionality'[36] – he contends that 'what we are calling emotions
proper at least involve both cognitions and feeling states where the
two are linked inasmuch as the former cause the latter'.[37] Emotions
are thus embodied, yet require a cognitive framework not only to be
understood, but even to be identified in the first place.

Again, there is a theological parallel here. A variety of forms of
theology carrying a 'post-liberal' label have corrected a view of theology which might suggest that a raw 'experience' comes first and
theology follows. Similarly, Carroll's cognitive psychological
approach to the film-watching experience indicates that emotional
responses are always located within a cognitive world. Though we
may, as viewers, be affected emotionally by some aspects of films
(Carroll gives the example of stomach-churning responses to car
chases), not all such reactions are 'emotions proper'. Emotions with
which we can actually work are those which can be cognitively
identified. I also feel them, however, in a bodily form. When I feel
fear (of something, of someone) I may shake, or go cold. When I am
shocked (by something, or someone) I may flinch, or recoil. When I
am attracted to someone, I may smile, or feel a tingling sensation.

Embodiment has not often been an agenda item for theologians.
For much of Christian history, for example, there has been greater
emphasis on negation of the body and its passions. Despite the doctrine of incarnation, Christianity does not have a good track record
of attending to bodies and flesh. Spirits and minds have been much
more prominent, particularly in Protestant traditions. It is thus
scarcely surprising that emotions too have been left under-
explored. Those aspects of human experience which are less

---

[35] Though seems to me undeveloped in Coates, *Romantic Legacy*.
[36] Carroll, 'Film, Emotion, and Genre', 25.
[37] Carroll, 'Film, Emotion, and Genre', 26.

conducive to systematic exposition – the givenness of the body, the potential uncontrollability of some emotions – have received considerably less attention.[38]

What could respect for the embodied nature of the film-watching experience contribute to theology's task? I suggest two things. First, the visceral nature of film-watching is in itself a challenge to many assumptions now being made about the 'screen culture' which we inhabit in the West. Cyberspace is often regarded as automatically liberating. Virtual communities are easily held to be preferable to communities which still face the hassles of actually meeting (and thus facing train delays, traffic jams, room hire, subsistence arrangements, checking on toilet facilities). However, '(f)lesh marks the very province of our humanity'.[39] The very fact that watching a film on video at home, or via a DVD player on computer, is less satisfying than viewing a film at a cinema on a big screen, in the company of others is instructive. 'Screen culture' is not uniform. It matters where our bodies are and amongst whom we place them through our embodied movement ('shall we go to the cinema or not?'). Theological reflection needs to take account of this, particularly with respect to its understanding of what forms of community/church sustain a theologically-informed approach to living.

Second, how we understand our own embodiment is crucial. Respect for the fact that we participate in a film-watching experience as embodied beings does not itself deliver a 'meaning'. Nor are our bodies somehow simply vehicles for, or receptacles of, a heap of emotions which we can acknowledge, and then 'work with'. One of the emphases of Graham's 2002 study is the way we construct our embodiment: '… while many commentators regard the liberating potential of disembodied cyberspace as Cartesian, they collapse too readily into a kind of dualism that associates embodiment with an unproblematic naturalism that evades the very constructedness and pluriformity of embodiment'.[40] In other words, whilst attention to the body challenges lazy conclusions about the potentialities of screen culture, it would be wrong to assume that we know what appeals to 'the body' amount to, or that all such appeals refer to a common understanding. It is part of the task of theological interaction with film, then, to offer an account of the embodied nature of film-watching. This is a constructive theological task which would inevitably draw on 'creatureliness', the givenness of the body, the sanctity of the body, but would need to offer such readings in a manner consistent with the film-watching experience.

---

[38] Except to be warned against and kept under control.
[39] Graham, *Representations*, 188.
[40] Graham, *Representations*, 189.

Such an exploration would then, in turn, provide a lens through which a viewer could re-evaluate portrayals of embodiment on screen. This would demonstrate quite clearly the dialogical nature of the interaction between theology/religion and film. My point here, however, is to put the emphasis more firmly on what arises from reflection upon the film-watching experience as an embodied experience than on the theme of films watched.

Visuality

The fourth heading under which I wish to draw together these critical reflections upon film-watching is 'visuality'. I borrow this term from Brent Plate, whose concern – to develop a 'religious visuality of film' – differs somewhat from my approach here. Plate is rightly critical of much theology/religion-film work for being too tied to models of interpretation drawn from literary studies.[41] The interdisciplinary approach to film-watching he seeks to develop wishes to pay greater respect to film *as film*, and he sees a need to focus less on popular film and more on avant-garde, experimental and independent (i.e. art house) film. He also pays attention to the physical experience of film-watching. He claims that this way of seeing would focus less on the theme of any film watched and more on the sensibility of the viewer. The viewer is, however, trained in watching film, rather than reading a book, or viewing a static image.

Plate's challenge is well made. I acknowledge the relevance of many of his criticisms to the project I was myself involved in back in the 1990s.[42] Many of the contributions focused on film themes alone, at a cost to respect of other dimensions of the film-watching experience. I am not, however, fully persuaded by all that Plate recommends, even whilst borrowing the term 'visuality' as one of the crucial headings at this point in my argument. The development of a 'discipline of seeing' in the manner proposed by Plate would, it seems to me, go too far towards merging aesthetics and religion.[43] Many different forms of art, art house films included, have their place in helping people develop new ways of seeing. But I am far from convinced that focusing on the aesthetics of seeing has any more guarantee of enabling people to 'begin to learn all over again how to love the other'.[44] Plate has, in other words, a laudable religious and ethical goal. But I need convincing that a more aesthetic (and ultimately more intellectual) approach to film-watching is

---

[41] Plate, 'Religion/Literature/Film', 17–19.
[42] Marsh and Ortiz (eds.), *Explorations*.
[43] Marsh and Ortiz (eds.), *Explorations* 31.
[44] Plate, 'Religion/Literature/Film', 35.

inevitably to be preferred to the rather different line I am adopting. My approach enters the more messy world of popular film, and seeks to work primarily from emotional responses than from attention to 'what is excluded in the frame, how does lighting, film stock, or camera angle affect the viewer's perception – and hence interpretation – of the person, places or things in the film'.[45]

This is not to say that Plate is not right to press those wishing to offer theological and religious readings of films to do more film studies homework. Indeed, much of what I have been able to explore in this book results from such work. But I am less convinced than Plate that such analysis will prove the primary and most fruitful channel through which 'new ways of seeing' will emerge *for most viewers*. Here is the crucial difference: I want to try and contribute to the development of strategies for thoughtful film-watching as part of ordinary living. I may be mistaken in thinking that ways of seeing are best worked out, therefore, in relation to popular film. And I accept that attention to art house films is undoubtedly more directly instructive about how films do what they do. But if theology and religious studies cannot find a way of connecting with the films that most people are watching, given that many such films clearly do have a huge cultural impact, then I would argue this is culturally worrying. It will not do to say that '(o)ne of the ways to change visual images ... is to pay attention to the images that do not merely promote the currently reigning cultural values',[46] as if 'currently reigning cultural values' are easily identifiable and able to be critiqued. Culture criticism is certainly part of theology's task, and will feature as an aspect of film studies, at its best. The more culturally influential approach, then, is to work with popular film and to devise ways of film-watching which do not merely accept 'the culturally reigning cultural values' they may contain, but work with viewers' responses to them in an accessible way. Theology will do well not simply to be prophetically critical, as it may need to be challenged by what films are actually doing to/for people, though it may choose to be (and give good reason for this) at times. But nor will this exercise be simply a matter of claiming theology's 'relevance'.

What, then, does my own version of 'visuality' amount to? 'Visuality' concerns a capacity for seeing. I am not here concerned to draw over-subtle distinctions between 'seeing' and 'really seeing', as if a spiritual message can be discerned in film (by a faithful few) which goes over and above what can be seen on screen. The theological reflection process I am seeking to construct around

---

[45] Plate, 'Religion/Literature/Film', 19.
[46] Plate, 'Religion/Literature/Film', 23.

the film-watching experience is more sensual and responsive than such a spiritualised reading would suggest. Visuality, as I understand it, is informed by film-critical ways of seeing. It clearly helps to be able to spot point of view shots, low camera angles, reaction shots, to know what a tracking shot is, or to interpret the significance of a bird's eye view shot. My concern, however, is to encourage the viewer to use such insights to enjoy film as a matter of course, rather than to develop any particularly 'religious' way of seeing. Such analytical tools should not be used ideologically in the service of a particular hermeneutic. Their use cannot ultimately be disinterested. But the ideological (religious, theological or other) use to which they are put is determined not by the tools themselves, but by the broader interpretative framework within which they are used. What I 'see' as a viewer is never simply a matter of what is on the screen, however well-honed my film-analytical skills may be.[47] But what I 'see' on the screen must nevertheless do justice to what the film and light show I am watching actually places before me. I interpret as I watch. But what appears on the screen before me constrains the range of meanings I can attach to it. I cannot make it mean simply what I want it to mean, even if the meaning I claim to glean from what I see on screen will not be the only possible 'reading' of the film.

Visuality, then, is about doing justice to what is physically presented in visual form. Stressing visuality in the context of considering a theological response to film-watching is salutary for two main reasons. First, it links with the wrestling which has occurred in different ways across religions with the question of whether (and if so, how) to portray the divine in pictorial form, and how, therefore, the visual arts more generally are to be evaluated.[48] Despite considerable suspicion about the visual arts, religions have usually found a place for their capacity to be vehicles of divine truth, at the intersection between human self-expression and encounter with the divine. For Christians, the visual arts at their best are to be understood sacramentally: as media which not only symbolise, but also mediate divine presence, thus constituting the continuing incarnation of God in the world. Films form a new challenge to this theology of art,

---

[47] And is always prone to the possibility of projection onto the screen image of what I want to 'see', a point at which this heading overlaps with the issues explored under 'illusions' above. Both illusion and visuality have strong subjective components: they entail the viewer does with what is 'there' (or which cinema makes us believe is 'there'). 'Visuality' concerns skills of seeing/interpreting, and thus puts more emphasis upon the viewer.

[48] C. Marsh, 'Religion and the Arts' in C. Partridge (ed.), *Dictionary of Contemporary Religion in the Western World*.

being a mass-produced medium, more elusive than static art, and requiring a language of interpretation which Christianity has not yet been able adequately to find or appropriate.[49] But locating them within the ongoing history of the theological appreciation of the visual arts (as opposed to treating them as vulgar entertainment, or demonic) means their theological potential has more chance of being acknowledged.

Second, attention to visuality in the reception of film reminds theology as a discipline that words have their limits. In this respect, films contribute to the contemporary challenge to the logocentrism of so much of Western (especially Protestant-influenced) culture. It is surely not coincidental that it is in the Roman Catholic tradition that the welcoming of film as a theological medium is more advanced.[50] Admittedly, this second point may play into the hands of critics of the entire theology/religion-film enterprise, who suspect that attention to film confirms both a dumbing down of theology (especially when it treats popular film) and a resulting lack of conceptual clarity in theology (when it is suggested that words fail). In response, the interplay of the features of film which are here being drawn out should be stressed. Visuality takes its place alongside a respect for emotion and embodiedness. What is being built up here is a picture of theology's working which is multi-sensual and has the chance of relating to the whole human person.

Again, the application of visuality – attending closely to what one sees on screen – to the watching of popular films is a crucial part of my approach. Viewers' close watching of films can thus become an aspect of 'ordinary theology'. Here I have considerable sympathy with Jeff Astley's exploration of this concept.[51] The arts as part of life are, however, strikingly absent from his treatment of ordinary theology. Chapter 6 will say more about how the combination of film-watching practices and responses I am exploring here a feature within ordinary theological practice.

Attentiveness

The encouragement to 'watch closely' brings me to my fifth and final feature of film-watching practice which carries theological

---

[49] M.E. Williams, 'Cinema', in A. Hastings, A. Mason and H. Pyper (eds.), *The Oxford Companion to Christian Thought*, 122.
[50] This has occurred despite the considerable concern, in Roman Catholicism too, about film's potential corrupting influence, and the continual involvement of religious groups in matters of censorship.
[51] J. Astley, *Ordinary Theology: Looking, Listening and Learning in Theology*.

resonance: attentiveness. Films command attention. In a cinema it is much harder to let one's attention wander than in a lounge. Large screen, surround sound and the company of others together facilitate concentration. All of these factors contribute to the viewer's immersion in and collusion with film's illusory qualities. But it is here where film-watching is at its most dangerous and its most revelatory: it is only because of the absorption, and the close watching which can accompany it, that films 'do' so much to people. Visuality, the triggering of emotional responses, and the enjoyment of the physicality of the experience (embodiment) all work together to sustain this absorption. The intensity of the film-watching experience, the stimulus for all of the reflections contained in this book is, however, both the cause of what makes it theologically so interesting, and the reason why reflection on it is both necessary and difficult. Expecting viewers to analyse their film-watching sounds like asking them to stifle their experience ('I only watched a film'; 'I only went for a night out'; 'I just wanted to be entertained'). But the concentration demanded by a well-made film invites the viewer to do more with it than their initial intention supposed.[52]

Attentiveness thus has two aspects to it. A good film commands a viewer's attention. Beyond the rapt attention of absorption in a film-watching experience, however, lies a different form of attentiveness: attention to the interplay between film and viewer, and exploration of the emotions, sensations and insights generated by the experience. Seen in these terms, attentiveness in film-watching is at the very least a therapeutic practice. Still more, it has the chance of being an exercise in practical theology. Watts and Williams, in their exploration of religious knowing and its parallels, pay particular attention to the concept of attentiveness.[53] Intriguingly, it is their chapter on attentiveness which highlights the importance of the emotional component in religious knowing, thus correlating emotional awareness and attentiveness in precisely the way in which I am suggesting needs to happen with film.

But what form is this broader attentiveness to take? Clearly it will involve a close, analytical attention to self – the emotions, senses, ideas and beliefs stimulated and brought into play as a result of an experience of watching a film. It will also require a locating of

---

[52] I do not, of course, want to claim that this is the case with every film. But I do not want to enter here into the question of what constitutes a good or bad film, or which are the films which most merit theological attention. This is simply not easy to predict, and is certainly not based solely on subject matter.

[53] F. Watts and M. Williams, *The Psychology of Religious Knowing*, chs. 5–6.

these reactions, in so far as one is able, within a cultural context. Attentiveness could become self-absorption if this process is not occurring. It is the practice of critical attentiveness which enables a viewer to move beyond film's illusory character, whilst respecting its appropriately illusory power. It is a means whereby watching *Iris* can be both an emotionally moving experience and an experience which takes me beyond the film. I am drawn into it not merely as something to think about. Through considering ageing parents, the complexity of demanding personal relationships with friends and relatives, and the emotional experience of confronting aspects of my own capacity to love and be enraged, I am taken beyond it. This is no mere intellectual exercise. In being attentive to all that watching the film requires of me – in my personal relationships, and through the process of reflection upon fidelity and fragility in relationship, human creativity, and the care of others – more than cognition is involved.

I cannot enter into this broader form of attentiveness, however, on the strength of the film-watching experience alone, or through mere introspection. I am required to locate myself socially and culturally, and to summon up the cognitive worlds and value systems within which I live my life (religion, politics, ethics, social class, sex and sexual orientation). All of these are not, of course, equally open to change. But all are tested in every life-experience. In the case of artistic encounter, for example, with a film, a cognitive process is begun which brings all such worlds and value systems to bear in the complexity of the viewing experience. Awareness of this, and working towards the articulation of this cognitive process, constitutes the attentiveness which makes the experience of watching a film so rich.

Beyond Cinematic Analogues: A Summary

I have sought, then, to characterise the film-watching experience under five headings: illusion, emotion, embodiment, visuality and attentiveness. I attached particular significance to the emotional component in film-watching, though have wanted to stress the interplay of this element with other aspects. I have sought to respect film as film, i.e. it is not music, or still art, or literature, though I know I will not have satisfied those who want greater attention to be paid to filmic technique in the task of interpreting film. My point has been to focus more on the interaction between film and viewer, without which talk of the 'film-watching experience' would not be possible. I have accepted film's illusory character: we know films are not 'real' but suspend disbelief in order to play their game. A twofold form of attentiveness, however, enables us both to immerse ourselves in the illusions which films create for the viewer, and to detach ourselves sufficiently from them in order to work out what they are doing to and for us. I have made some mention of religious and theological concerns in exploring the five headings. The main work of drawing out the theological significance of what I have undertaken here, however, is the subject of the next chapter.

Case-Study D

The Lure of the Director: Films of the Coen Brothers

Theology is a communal enterprise and seems to function best when related directly to specific religious communities or traditions. As such it often has an unattributable aspect to it: church reports, for example, do not usually indicate which parts were written by whom. When agreed by Synods, Houses of Bishops, or church conferences, and then published, they are collectively owned. But the individual authors are often hidden, their names lost in lists of committee-members or working party contributors.

Individual theologians do, of course, have their own thoughts, their own disputes with their own (and others') tradition, and write books revealing their own distinct emphases. On the British scene in the present it is true, for what seems the first time in a long while, that there are people – not only inside churches – waiting for theological works to appear. They await the arrival of 'the latest Rowan Williams' in their nearest bookshop. This is not often the case outside of limited theological circles. Williams writes as an individual who happens also to be an archbishop, and presumably has to ask himself when he writes about the relationship between the form of orthodoxy he espouses and the church he represents.

Directors are (slightly) like individual theologians. They have none of the obvious ideological limitations which being a bishop may entail, though what they envision in the making of their films may be far from what ends up appearing on screen. The demands of production, budget constraints, the work of editors, the requirements of distributors, together with the results of trial screenings all obscure directorial intention and function as constraints on the vision of individuals. Furthermore, directors differ in the extent to which they control their actors and welcome suggestions and alterations to the screenplay or a proposed scene. Only the most rigorous form of auteur theory, or the knowledge that a particular director works in a meticulous, hands-on way with their cast and crew, can make a simple equation between a director and an individual theologian. That said, directors are like theologians to the extent that for film-watchers, particular directors can draw the crowds ('this is a Francis Ford Coppola film', a Scorsese, a Woody Allen, a Jane Campion film, a Robert Altman movie). Regardless of who the stars are, or whether there are even stars at all, some directors' films will usually be worth a look.

But what does this feature of film-watching contribute to the cinema-going habit? I propose to address the question using the Coen Brothers' films as a test-case. They provide an interesting example as they are very 'hands-on', and dislike making changes to their carefully crafted screenplays. They are often referred to as 'quirky', indicating that they have a distinct style. They also operate in the borderlands between popular and art-house films, have directed commercially successful (though not blockbuster) films and have, most recently, ventured directly into mainstream movies with *Intolerable Cruelty* (2003).[1]

How, then, does the following of a particular director's works shape a cinema-goer's film-watching habit? Interaction with the Coen brothers' oeuvre suggests that four insights can be drawn. First, an emerging body of work leads a viewer to become familiar with a particular artistic style. The Coens thrive on their unpredictability. But this unpredictability becomes winsome and is one of the main reasons that viewers who watch 'a Coen brothers film' keep on returning. This aspect of cinema-going thus relates to a general consideration in interpretation about ways of reading. 'Readers' of film simply become familiar with distinct ways in which directors present their material. In the case of the Coen brothers, they demand much of their viewers (who need to pay attention throughout). But this both sharpens a viewer's sensitivity to the Coen brothers' own style, and in turn makes viewers more attentive in general as film-watchers.

Second, the Coen brothers' films provide an excellent reminder of the fact that viewers are to do more with their films than simply watch them. They are clearly to be enjoyed, and humour – even if of a rather dark form – is a consistent feature throughout their films. But *Raising Arizona* (1987) *Fargo* (1996) and *O Brother, Where Art Thou?* (2000), to cite three examples, are clearly able to do more than merely provide an evening's entertainment. Mark

---

[1] Their full list of films to date comprises *Blood Simple* (1983), *Raising Arizona* (1987), *Miller's Crossing* (1990), *Barton Fink* (1991), *The Hudsucker Proxy* (1994), *Fargo* (1995), *The Big Lebowski* (1997), *O Brother, Where Art Thou?* (2000), *The Man Who Wasn't There* (2001), and *Intolerable Cruelty* (2003).

Stibbe's popular treatment of *Fargo* may find Christian themes too easily in relation to the film, but his point stands that it is 'like a post-modern morality tale'.[2] The Coen brothers clearly want to provoke, though not merely in the short-term. Every film raises moral questions. And the manner in which the films raise moral questions accentuates a point which could be made abstractly or analytically (moral questions are not always easily answered), but without the same emotional power or ordinary complexity which the Coen brothers' films present.[3] To take *Raising Arizona* as an example: though classifiable as a 'delirious mix of slapstick, surrealism and sentimentality',[4] the film invites the viewer to consider the intense impact of childlessness upon a couple wanting children and the possibility of reform for a repeat offender.[5] The viewer is lured into feeling sympathy for a couple who kidnap a child, one of a set of quintuplets born to the wife of a ruthless, self-made furniture salesman. This sympathy is accentuated by the lack of sympathy the viewer is intended, at one level of response, to feel for the parents of the quintuplets. The degree of ultimacy entailed in the kidnap of the child is, however, dealt with humorously, though also quasi-religiously, through the Coen brothers' secularisation of religious motif. The 'lone biker of the apocalypse' pursues the couple, keeping alive in stark symbolic form the question of how the depth of accountability for moral actions is to be understood and represented.

Not all directors, of course, will necessarily have the aim of, or succeed in, stimulating the viewer to 'work with' a film beyond the occasion of its viewing. Indeed, the extent to which this appears not to be the aim of so many films means some theologians and scholars of religion are surprised that so much attention is paid to film. An important point here, however, is that directors do have intentions, and sometimes these remain evident in and through a film and cohere with theological interests and purposes, even if those intentions are very diverse and not overtly religious or theological.

The deft handling of moral issues in films of the Coen brothers indicates a third aspect of attention to watching particular

---

[2] J. John and M. Stibbe, *The Big Picture: Finding the Spiritual Message in Movies*, 74.

[3] By 'ordinary complexity' I mean that the Coen brothers translate into humorous, sometimes surreal, but nevertheless accessible locations and scenes a complex moral question or set of questions which watchers are drawn into considering in an interesting and entertaining way.

[4] Fane-Saunders, *Radio Times Guide to Films*, 1173.

[5] The cinematic links between *Raising Arizona* and *The Shawshank Redemption* are worth mentioning in relation to the latter theme.

directors' films. Not only does such viewing of a particular director's films increase film literacy through familiarity, it also reminds
viewers that directors, too, have ideological frameworks within
which they work. The ideological framework (of needing to make
money) of the funding and distribution of a film is far from the sole
framework shaping the viewer's experience. Directors may say they
have no other purpose than to fill a few hours of their viewers' time
in an entertaining way, but at least they do have intentions. And
they have backgrounds, values and ideological persuasions too. The
Coen brothers are playful here. They often seek to play down their
affluent origins, or the significance of their formal education (Joel in
film, Ethan in philosophy). Yet inevitably their work is a product of
critical reflection upon both. They are from a Jewish family. The
impact of Judaism upon their work could itself be worth closer scrutiny. Though less overt an element than in the work of Woody
Allen, their preoccupation with tough moral questions, with ambiguity, with people being not what they seem, with the depths of
human goodness and evil may not result solely from a willingness to
ask questions about life.

Fourth, the Coen brothers' work provides an excellent example
of films which both flirt with the sentimental and subvert it. *Raising
Arizona* and *Intolerable Cruelty* are scarcely classifiable as
'weepies'. But they touch on basic issues in domestic life (parenting
and marriage) around which many films of a sentimental nature are
produced. Their handling of the subject-matter makes customary
use of the unexpected to prevent viewers from predicting plot
twists, and thus to trust their own knee-jerk reactions to characters
and situations. In the process, emotional responses to everyday
issues – even if presented to the viewer in unusual contexts – are
exposed. The viewer is invited to be self-critical as part of the activity of watching the film.

By choosing to watch a particular director's films, then, a cinema-goer engages in a conversation with an artist, just as if he or she
were awaiting the latest novel by a favourite writer. Despite the constraints of film production, directors' visions do find their way onto
screen. The interactive process of interpretation that occurs
between viewer and film is less direct than that which occurs
between a reader and a novelist's text. Its occurrence in the context
of the multi-sensual experience of film-watching may mean that the
director remains even more hidden than a novelist. The interpretative process begun by a viewer's reception of a director's work can,
however, become a major way in which a viewer thinks about life.

6

Film-Watching as a Theological Practice

Five main threads have run through this book.[1] The first is a concentration upon *film as a social practice*.[2] I have sought to explore the significance of film as a medium around which a set of social habits form. It was upon this basis that the first chapter was possible at all. Only through recognising the fact that, by virtue of being shown in public, a film automatically becomes a site of mass consumption and social engagement is it possible also to look at parallels between cinema-going and religious practice.

This insight also lay behind the explorations in Chapter 2. The social nature of film-watching inevitably presses the case for examining the similarity and contrast between audiences and congregations. The precise nature of the practices of these two gathered groups needed distinguishing carefully. It is nevertheless clear that, for many people, film-watching is fulfilling some of the functions in relation to living that religious people find met in the context of worship. That this is so became clear in the ensuing chapters. Chapters 3 to 5 show that it is neither merely film as a medium, nor the content of particular films, which may support films' functioning as resources in the context of a religious or quasi-religious set of practices but also their actual reception.

I have, however, not overlooked *how films work in themselves*. The attention here has not been simply on their narratives or themes, but on strategies the films use to draw attention to aspects of their content, and to arouse particular responses from their viewers. In following this approach I have been trying to avoid two false extremes. On the one hand, I have been seeking to resist a textual determinacy about film, according to which a film's meaning is located either in the 'form' by which it is constructed, or

---

[1] Though some of these threads do link more clearly with one chapter than another, all threads interweave within each chapter.
[2] For an illuminating exploration of this theme from a film studies perspective, see Turner, *Film as Social Practice*.

in its subject-matter alone ('literature with pictures', in Turner's delightful phrase[3]). On the other hand, I have been trying to resist the most common failing of participants in the theology/religion-film debate, namely to imply that theological meaning is *in* a film simply awaiting the discovery of trained theological interpreters, when in reality theological meaning is brought almost entirely *to* a film, as if the film has no claim at all on the interpreter.

In order to conduct the exploration so far, I have been operating with a *functional understanding of religion*. Rather than raise questions of meaning (whether interim or ultimate) or truth, I have proceeded heuristically, testing out whether or not film-watching as practice in any way relates to religion as practice. The emphasis upon practice and practices, however, shelves many questions. For the enquiry to move beyond the 'merely interesting', as a sociological observation, and to carry any broader cultural or theological weight, then more will have to be said about the nature of religion and theology. Theology may (quite rightly) not reclaim its place as the 'Queen of Sciences' or make any lazy claim to have access to some supreme meaning. But it cannot make do with functional theories alone. It has to be interested in truth, however difficult that interest is to carry through.

Fourth, I have laid particular emphasis throughout upon the *emotional aspect* of film-watching. Recognising that emotional triggers and responses were crucial in both of the highly successful films I considered in detail, I shall now relate the importance of this discovery to theology's task. This will entail a review of the explorations of the first two chapters in light of the discovery. What is to be made of the importance of the emotional for theology, worship and religion as a social practice? Does this amount to any more than a confirmation – from a different area of cultural life – of what some Christian groups are claiming, i.e. that we need more emotionally-charged worship? As I shall show, the importance of the emotional – for film-watching and theology – needs locating within the range of other aspects of the social practice of each. But its intrinsic power should not be stunted in the process.

Fifth, I have suggested that watching popular film is particularly significant because of the role played by *sentimentality*. Rather than conclude that sentiment always descends into mawkishness, I have sought to explore the importance of apparent resort to emotional excess. This is a tricky conclusion to come to, but it is the hinge of my whole thesis. To express my view at its simplest: if theology is to be part of life, then it must find ordinary channels along which to

---

[3] Turner, *Film as Social Practice*, 46.

run. Film-watching (including even the watching of popular films) can come close to being identified as an explicitly theological activity. If the watching of popular films entails sentimentality, then so be it; theology must find out how to handle the sentimental.[4] This will not mean that anything sentimental is religiously useful. It simply alerts theology to the fact that if it is to consider examination of the affective dimension of human living as part of its brief, then it cannot ignore what is often too quickly defined culturally as 'the sentimental'. I think it is even fair to say that it would be better for theology to risk the charge of being interested in 'kitsch', than to be accused of other-worldliness, as it undertakes its task.[5]

---

[4] Frank Burch Brown's point, made with reference to religious art, is, however, pertinent: 'When it comes to religious art, I am prepared to argue that there is room both for sentiment and sentimentality, and thus for easy emotion and a kind of indulgence. That is true for many of the same reasons that Christians should be allowed or perhaps encouraged occasionally to revisit, nostalgically, feelings associated with a quite uncritical phase of love, with naïve sympathy, or with a state of unabashed wonder. Sometimes indulging in easy emotion will open up a capacity to feel more deeply, when that is called for. (Adults whose hearts have been strangely warmed by the bedtime stories they have read to children know this can happen, and how valuable it can be.) But when sentimentality dominates the religious space, it truncates religious development, at least in the aesthetic sphere. To acknowledge that sentimental and otherwise "defective" religious art has its place is not to forget the importance of evaluation but to recognise that various criteria enter into religious aesthetic judgment' (F.B. Brown, *Good Taste, Bad Taste, and Christian Taste: Aesthetics in Religious Life*, 20). Brown's is one of the few theological works to tackle directly the kinds of issues I am addressing here, though he is more heavily focussed on an explicitly religious context for art/the arts, and on worship throughout. He offers twelve assumptions for 'testing Christian taste' (Brown, *Good Taste*, 250–1).

[5] Brown has a good chapter on kitsch (Brown, *Good Taste*, 128–59). There is little doubt that handling the sentimental dimension of popular films comes close to dealing with 'predictable responses' and 'emotional reflexes' in viewers. But as Brown himself notes: 'Reflexive emotional responses are not all bad...nor is guarded sensibility always good' (Brown, *Good Taste*, 146). Ultimately, whilst '(d)iscipline and training does not guarantee superiority...it does open up possibilities that are otherwise unavailable' (Brown, *Good Taste*, 158). In the case of this present book, this entails teasing out what makes for good and bad films, and how such judgments interweave with spiritual and moral development. Late in the process of writing this book I came across Mark Wallinger's judgment on Bill Viola's art: '... he's the Billy Graham of the art world – all that emoting...Unbelievably kitsch' (cited in F. Guner, 'The artist ascending' in *The Independent*, 14 January 2003, Arts Section, 15). The correlation of

I must now, though, dig deeper to establish what happens to theology on the basis of this enquiry. If a functional understanding of religion is not likely to be enough to do justice to theology's truth-enquiring task, then how can theology make use of film? And if, within an appropriation and critical examination of film's social and cultural function, as much is to be made of the emotional and sentimental aspects of film as I am suggesting, where does this leave theology?

The Critical Function of Theology

Theology has a critical role to play in contemporary culture. I use the word 'critical' in two senses. Theology has an analytical-evaluative role, both within religion/religions and also in relation to wider culture. To cite Christianity as an example, Christian theology is the discipline which keeps alive Christianity's capacity for self-critique and its openness to critique from outside. In wider culture, theology is one of the disciplines which constantly demands that cultures look critically at themselves, offering resources and evaluations of what is happening in society for public attention and scrutiny. The theological examination of the practice of film-watching is thus located in both of these worlds. Discussion of films enables religious traditions to look at how they are portrayed in wider culture. It also enables religions to see a version of the issues and values dominant in society. That same discussion can also be a context in which religious beliefs are brought to bear in relation to what films present. In the latter case, it is admittedly not surprising that talk of 'theology-film dialogue' has sometimes come simply to mean religions' response to what 'the world' believes, as presented through film. This is to over-simplify. But there is no doubt that without a sense of the dialogical character of the interaction between the world of theology and film, the mutually critical function of both worlds does not have a chance to develop.[6]

---

[5] (*continued*) emotion with kitsch thus seems easy to draw and suggests that attention to 'art' may leave this aspect of being human under-explored. I suggest this is exactly what is happening in many explorations of 'theology and the arts'.

[6] In reality, as this book has demonstrated, the 'dialogue' is a complex conversation between many conversation-partners: film-directors, screenplay writers, film editors, film critics, film studies writers, cinema owners, sociologists, psychologists, cultural critics, systematic theologians, practical or pastoral theologians, liturgists, worship-leaders, to name but a few. On this point, I am puzzled by the simple dichotomising (and effective dismissal) of dialogical approaches to film in relation to the world of theology

Theology has a critical role to play, however, in a second sense. It has a role to play at this present (critical) time in Western culture's development. Most cultures have phases when they feel in crisis. We need not over-dramatise the West's particular, current version of this. But a number of features of contemporary culture can be drawn together to suggest that a major rethink about some of its tendencies might be worthwhile. Six features present themselves.[7] First, an individualism stemming from the Renaissance, or from the Reformation, or the Enlightenment, or twentieth-century existentialism, or the 1960s (all are possible contenders as initiators) has come to a head in the late-, or post-, modern world we now inhabit. Individual autonomy has priority over relatedness or accountability to a community. Second, despite the emphasis on the individual, the individual self is disappearing. Because of contemporary emphasis upon the individual's construction of his or her self, and an opposition to the notion that there is any 'essence' to being human, the level of demand upon individuals to 'make something of themselves' has increased enormously. Third, the way that people seek to 'make something of themselves' is often linked with the capacity to consume. The dominance of consumption as a human practice in Western culture has thus become an issue about identity: we are what we consume in the sense that 'lifestyle choice' (for those with the means and the freedom to choose, of course) means 'identity choice'. Fourth, society has fragmented. This argument exists in a nostalgic form ('things are not what they were', 'you used to know your neighbours') which can be challenged. But the argument is difficult to dispute when social mobility, speed of travel, and the impact of technology upon the way that people relate to each other are taken into account. More than ever, communities now cut across the neighbourhoods, villages, towns and cities where people live. A fragmented society has come to mean a very differently networked society. Fifth, Western culture is secularised, but religion persists.[8] The rather vigorous forms of secularism of the 1960s and

---

[6] *(continued)* over against his own approach to 'cinematic theology' by Gerard Loughlin. Though Loughlin's approach may imply a more sophisticated understanding of 'culture' and theology's inevitable embeddedness within it (in the sense that theology cannot detach itself as easily as the language of dialogue implies), one is left then wondering how any sort of critical function for theology is possible at all. I return to this later in the chapter.

[7] Many of these are considered, even if a different way, in Marsh, *Christianity in a Post-Atheist Age*.

[8] On different kinds of secularisation, see e.g. Marsh, *Christianity in a Post-Atheist Age*, 21–6.

1970s have been found wanting, and may have contributed to some ill-informed versions of religion emerging in the relative vacuum which followed those decades. But the secularisation thesis, according to which religions should have been found out and disappeared by now, has proved inadequate. Sixth, religion has to account for itself at a time when the close alliance between religion and violence seems difficult to dispute. The 'close alliance' is one which can both promote violence (violent acts perpetrated in the name of God/religion) and oppose it. All religions are associated with violence because they strive to be pathways of peace, in the sense that they encourage people to face everything in themselves that would draw them towards violence. Most religions also seek to identify a transcendent source in relation to which violence can be faced and resources found to resist it and transform those who perpetrate it. In Christianity, then, the symbol of the cross serves as a reminder that all people live in a world prone to violence. The cross is also a symbol of hope when linked with resurrection, and thus viewed within the light of God's participation in the world. But without this wider theological perspective, the cross cannot function as a symbol of peace and hope.

In no way do I suggest that this six-sided sketch of contemporary culture is exhaustive or comprehensive. But I suggest that these are nevertheless crucial features of the cultural time in which theology currently seeks to operate. This is the contemporary 'crisis' (critical time) therefore. If theology is to find its appropriate role, and if sense is to be made of theology's function within the task of understanding the role and 'consumption' of film in Western culture, then it must find its role in relation to such features as these.

Contested (But Essential) Concepts

Theology as Tradition

Theology is often identified simply as a body of knowledge (a tradition). Christian theology can then be 'learned', like the periodic table of chemical elements. This is a very static understanding of the concept of 'tradition' but is important nevertheless. There is a cognitive aspect to the theological task which entails drawing upon a body of knowledge. The insights of cognitive psychology, as we have seen, prove helpful in understanding how people 'process' their responses to film. What psychologists have shown to be the case carries over into theology in two ways. It serves as a reminder of the cognitive dimension in all human experience and it reveals the complex processing involved in human experience. It is with respect to the former aspect, I suggest, which the theological reception of film has much to contribute to film studies and with regard to the latter that it has much to contribute to theology. In other words, theology joins forces with cognitive psychology in a suspicion of appeal to 'raw experiences' or unfocussed emotions. Theology is one of many disciplines which note that all human experience is located within frameworks of interpretation. As such it contributes to developments now occurring within film studies itself.[9] In its quest to be truly true interdisciplinary, film studies must not overlook the contribution that religious studies and theology can make. Conversely, as films *require* multi-sensual and multi-perspectival thinking and feeling, theology as a discipline is reminded that it must relate to the whole person, and not simply the head.

Realism and Non-Realism

For theology to function as a cognitive world, though, of course, does not require God to exist. There are plenty of people who find the history of religion fascinating, informative and even existentially illuminating and do not believe in God. A book which tackles the topic of the theological reception of film must therefore accept that such reception is still going to prove possible amongst many for whom 'God as (a) reality' will be a non-issue. At this point, I am not going to try to argue for the existence of God! All that need be said is that the distinction between realism and non-realism in theology is an important one. For realists, God is. There is an independent reality to which the word 'God' refers, the clarification of whose identity and the living according to whose ways is ultimately the 'point' of theology. For non-realists, the word 'God' denotes ultimate values, but is a necessary linguistic means by which such values are grasped in what may be termed 'posited transcendence'. We must, then, live 'as if' the values we have constructed and chosen are given to us, in a way which is both dangerous (through the absolutisation of values) and yet essential (we are saying more than simply 'this is how we'd like to live'). Both of these groups are to be distinguished from agnostics and atheists.[10]

Stressing the two types of approach to theology is significant not only for explanatory purposes. There is an apologetic purpose at

---

[9] '(I)t is possible to argue that film studies have broken with aesthetics in order to reconnect films with their audiences, film-makers with their industries, film texts with society' (Turner, *Film as Social Practice*, 206).
[10] The unknowability of God for agnostics means, in practice, that the term or concept of God may carry little practical significance. For atheists, use of the term 'God' is misguided altogether. Some regard it as dangerous.

work here. In suggesting that film studies would benefit from a broader interdisciplinary base, I am also stressing that a value can be found for religious studies and theology not only by those who feel able to make particular types of metaphysical claims about God. Indeed, I would go much further: unless ways can be found to enable those who do not profess any explicit religious belief to discover the value of encounter with theological resources, then the development of Western culture will be all the poorer.

In 2002 I wrote these words:

> ... Agnostic onlookers and theological non-realists must not be excluded from the Christian search for God. Indeed, it should be accepted that they are likely already to be an integral part of organized Christianity. They should be welcomed in Christian communities. We are, in all probability, always shifting positions anyway, even those of us who profess a firm(-ish) faith. So to include amongst the community (or communities) of faith those who are still trying to find faith should not be a surprise.

> My guess that there are many *de facto* agnostics and non-realists sitting in churches week in and week out is not merely an expression of hope. It is more a reflection on the evident questioning and searching that people do in private, or in contexts other than in the life of the church.[11]

The pertinence of this insight to what is actually happening in and around Christian communities seems clearer to me now than ever. Churches are not simply full of committed believers. All sorts of people with very many kinds of faith, many images and understandings of God, vastly diverse spiritualities and hugely differing levels of commitment, are involved with churches. In cinemas, I suggest, is an even greater diversity of people (of all religions and none). But there is more overlap and interaction with the realist and non-realist cognitive world of theology than people will often have the opportunity or context to explore. Churches are often not places where film-watching is or could be discussed. A broader social and cultural question thus arises: where could a film-viewer go to reflect on the emotional/aesthetic/cognitive experience which cinema-going experience appears to be?

Communities and Narratives
This leads to a third important area of exploration: the relationship between theology understood as a tradition and the question of how such a tradition is 'carried'. It is all very well to claim that

---

[11] Marsh, *Christianity in a Post-Atheist Age*, 110.

cinema-goers, film-critics and film studies lecturers may benefit from deeper immersion in the cognitive world of theology, but how is this to happen, and to happen appropriately, unless they actually belong to a religious community of some sort? For are not theologies in religions largely carried in narrative form? And is not the task of carrying the narratives (and re-interpreting primary narratives/scriptures) a crucial task of embodied communities?

It is here where one of the crucial difficulties, but also profound insights, of the critical dialogue between theology and film occurs. The habit of cinema-going creates a whole series of temporary 'communities' for a cinema-goer. The films watched present a range of narrative worlds within which the cinema-goer is invited to participate. A kind of uniformity of worldview may be presented if only Hollywood films are watched. A sort of continuity of experience may be felt if the same multiplex is visited. But it is far from the sense of 'community' which religions at their best can create. The sense of 'inhabiting' a tradition which religious practice can bring is thus far from the practice of cinema-going per se.

However, the cognitive processing which occurs in the practice of film-watching does invite consideration of which cognitive worlds a film-goer *will* draw upon and whether or not these will include anything drawn from religion. What is more, the multi-sensual, multi-perspectival experience which film-watching is, as was explored in chapter 2, provides a major challenge to religious communities to consider the forms in which a narrative tradition may be best received and worked with.

Cinema-goers thus participate in a communal experience in a radically different way from those who are committed to religious communities. Those who are 'members' of *both* types of communities are likely to prioritise their religious practice over other types of communal belonging, in so far as their religious commitments are likely to shape other life-practices. More crucially, the fact must be respected that all cinema-goers and all religiously committed people in fact belong to a whole range of communities (work groups, families, friends, political groups, leisure clubs). All of these make claims upon them in terms of time-demands, the emotion of people's association with them, and the exposure to the cognitive worlds (and values) which 'belonging' entails. The value system of a particular family, for example, may very rarely be articulated, and still less explored. But it will be very powerfully conveyed through a family's practice.

And here's the rub. An 'associational', networked, style of living – typical of a fragmented, technologically oriented, postmodern culture – accentuates an individualistic approach to participation in diverse cognitive worlds: you pick up what you can, where you can, be it at church, cinema, pub, concert arena, sports stadium. The question of coherence beyond the 'collecting' (of experiences and insights) arises. And above all the question arises of where and how an individual might have a chance to explore the results of all this bewildering variety of cases of cognitive processing. For this process of reflecting on experience is not only, as both film-watching and churchgoing show conclusively, a cognitive matter.

Theology as a Multi-Dimensional Habit

Theology is therefore to be understood as a multi-dimensional habit, a way of living with a number of aspects to it. There are four main, interlocking dimensions: aesthetic, affective, cognitive and ethical (I list them alphabetically, not in any order or priority). The aesthetic dimension develops a person's sensibilities to beauty through the senses. This dimension is clearly a crucial part of the film-watching experience, too, especially with respect to sight and sound. The fact is that both 'good' and 'bad' films (from an aesthetic or technical point of view) may have something to offer theology. But theologians may do well to develop their aesthetic sensibilities so that they are at least aware what might constitute a 'good' or 'bad' film in this sense, even if they may not wish to be constrained in their theological interests by the aesthetic judgment of film critics. As in relation to all engagement with the arts, however, it must be possible for theologians to learn much about 'ways of seeing' from those who have few, if any, explicit theological interests at all.

The affective dimension is the one I have emphasised throughout this book. Stressing the interaction which occurs between film and viewers in the film-watching process, I have sought to emphasise the way in which the context of viewing, the emotional triggers in film, and the viewers' responses on many levels (not least cognitive and affective) get to work within the viewer's processing of the film-watching experience. It is for this reason, too, that I have wanted to suggest a more positive role for so-called 'sentimentality'. This should prove, rightly, a contentious part of my argument because it is fraught with potential misunderstanding and misleading consequences. At its most crass it may sound as if I am suggesting that any old junk may prove a theological resource. This is because, at root, I am suggesting that anything *can*. Sentimentality is, however, no more a guarantee of theological usefulness than aesthetic brilliance or even philosophical profundity. My purpose in signalling a potential value to sentimentality in film is threefold. First, it resists an ever-present tendency in theology to gravitate towards 'real art', as if popular culture has little to offer theology.[12] Second, it links with more recent approaches in film studies which look at what films actually do, rather than what is in them and what it is assumed they should do. Third, it reminds us of the sheer power and frequent unexpectedness of the range of emotional responses which films can arouse.

This attention to theology's affective dimension connects with theology's interest in 'feeling'. Friedrich Schleiermacher's famous, even notorious, definition of true religion as a 'sense and taste for the infinite' and his characterisation of the pious consciousness as a 'feeling of absolute dependence' are crucial here.[13] Often criticised for reducing all religion and theology to mere self-expression, or to inner states, Clements' interpretation of Schleiermacher's approach is incisive and accurate:

> ... while Schleiermacher speaks of the religious feeling as a self-consciousness, it is clear that this cannot mean simply a 'consciousness of oneself' without reference to any reality other than oneself. The self-consciousness of which Schleiermacher speaks is a consciousness of the self as determined by, or acted upon by, what is other than the self, as well as its own inwardly motivated actions. It is the self-in-relation which is the object of consciousness ... It is the self grounded in a realm of what is other than self, of other persons, the realm of nature and society, the whole finite realm grounded in the Infinite, which Schleiermacher is concerned with. The human consciousness is thus never entirely self-awareness, for the self can never be extracted from the realm of otherness.[14]

The affective dimension of theology thus respects the power of the emotions in human life without reducing theology to the expression or articulation of those emotions. Theology is, of course, more likely to face the charge of not respecting the emotional at all, given its preference for rationality. This occurs when it is not seen as a discipline relating to the whole person, and when largely disconnected from worship. The film-theology dialogue helps here on both fronts.

I have already considered the cognitive dimension of theology ('Theology as Tradition'). In no sense do I wish to play down this

---

[12] Plate picks up my stereotypically Protestant concern about elitism in Plate, 'Religion/Literature/Film', 37 n.19, cf. Marsh, 'Film and Theologies of Culture', 31–2.

[13] F.D.E. Schleiermacher, *On Religion: Speeches to Its Cultured Despisers*, 35, cited in K. Clements, *Friedrich Schleiermacher: Pioneer of Modern Theology*, 85; F.D.E. Schleiermacher, *The Christian Faith*, 16, cited in Clements, *Schleiermacher*, 103.

[14] Clements, *Schleiermacher*, 37.

aspect of theology in commending attention to films' emotional impact and the cognitive processing which occurs around the emotional-aesthetic stimulus which films create in the viewer. My argument is simply that theological attention to what can happen when people watch films reminds theologians to put theology's different dimensions into appropriate perspective.

Finally, theology's ethical dimension must be considered. If anything, this is the dimension of the theological task which is played down in this book. Again, this is in no sense because it is the least significant. It is simply not the immediate focus when the task of exploring what happens in film-watching is under scrutiny. An ethical dimension is, of course, at work even there too. People are reacting – as part of the cognitive processing going on – to ethical standpoints portrayed on screen, and via considerations of whether they do or do not identify with characters presented. I have, however, resisted this as a main line of enquiry in this book for one simple reason: I wanted to offer an alternative to a common tendency to use films to deal with 'issues'. This has been a feature of some work in the religion/theology-film dialogue. It also features widely in education in many forms (e.g. in personal and social development education in schools, in philosophy). Whilst it is undeniable that films often deal directly (and very helpfully) with 'issues', the problem with such an approach is the same as when interpreters try and say 'the theology in this film is …'. It does not account sufficiently for films as films, and for the interplay between a film and its viewers. Nevertheless, there can be no question that film-watching contributes in a variety of ways to viewers' always-developing ethical standpoints. In this way, the practice of film-watching locates itself within the range of dimensions of theology's task.

All of these dimensions of theology need to be explored in social contexts. There is no theology without reference to a community of tradition which 'carries' theology's cognitive world, and to specific communities of practice in which the interpretation of that tradition is appropriated and reworked. In such specific communities, the reworking constantly interweaves with other cognitive worlds (politics, ethics, philosophy, culture) as well as theology's other three dimensions, as represented in both the individual lives of community members, and in the communities' lives together. In Christian terms, this is a reminder that theology always relates to church and churches. The contemporary challenge, however, is to acknowledge the fact that churches in the West in the present are often weak (numerically, religiously, spiritually, aesthetically, liturgically, intellectually) and the notion that this multidimensional approach to theology has a chance of being sustained in such communities thus becomes farfetched. Such a conclusion cannot, however, alter the fact that theology needs communal bases to relate to. Theology cannot be an isolated discipline. No one can ultimately be a religious believer, or any kind of theologian, by themselves. Even though people clearly do 'pick 'n' mix their spirituality, the question arises as to how such individualism and the social fragmentation that inevitably accompanies it are sustainable. The possibility of churches (and religious groupings in other traditions) reasserting themselves and strengthening their communal life is one option. The possibility of their doing something with films, in order to revivify their theological and communal life, is another. There also exists the possibility that film theatres and multiplexes might, in fact, have a much bigger social and educational role to play than they recognise.

Theology, Spirituality, Life

I have avoided until now exploring one further, final crucial concept in this enquiry, without which a contemporary examination of the impact and theological reception of film would be incomplete. I refer to the concept of 'spirituality'. As has rightly been said recently:

> 'Spirituality' is a term much in vogue: it sounds significant, with a touch of mystery, seeming to allow escape from the intellectual quest and wearisome wrestling with mental problems. We turn with relief from theology to spirituality, but may find ourselves enmeshed in a bewildering variety of techniques, or excitedly following a trail leading nowhere.[15]

That said, we cannot avoid the term. For there is little doubt that in the present cultural climate in the West, religion is a more unacceptable reality than spirituality. Religion implies structure and institution (and for some is off-putting for that very reason). It has also come to mean constraint, oppression, even abuse. Spirituality, by contrast, means freedom, autonomy, self-expression, the development of body and soul.[16] That the two should have been prised so far apart is frankly astonishing (especially when those going in search of a spirituality so often draw on ages-old religious material). Confirmation that this has happened, however, can be found in every main chain bookstore, in which, alarmingly, 'Religion' and 'Mind, Body, Spirit' constitute two entirely separate sections.

---

[15] G. Wakefield, 'Spirituality, Forms of', in A. Hastings, A. Mason and H.Pyper (eds.), *The Oxford Companion to Christian Thought*, 685.
[16] Marsh, *Christianity in a Post-Atheist Age*, 29–30.

The experience of film-watching is an exercise in spirituality. I do not use the term 'religious experience' as that would require a closer definition of that further concept than I would want to offer, and potentially label the film-watching experience in too restrictive a way. By calling film-watching 'an exercise in spirituality' I am signifying two things. First, it relates to a person's inner life, in whatever way that term 'inner life' is understood. Whether a person laughs or cries, gets angry, or is shocked, film works on the inner life. Second, film-watching (especially in its cinema-going form) is not usually just an incidental activity. It may not be a weekly ('ritual') practice, but it is often special or significant to a viewer. It thus takes some place within a person's life-structure. It is thus in this sense that I wish to speak of film-watching in relation to spirituality: as a contribution to work on the inner life, in the context of a life-structure.

When seen in this manner, the contemporary (positive) approach to spirituality, alongside the commonly (negative) approach to religion take on a fresh light. Film-watching, despite usually having a communal element to it, does not in fact make much of this. Unless undertaken in an educative setting in which the context of watching is explored as part of the experience, the film-watching experience is largely detached from any ensuing exploration of a film, except in so far as it relates to the reception of a film *by individuals*. This phenomenon relates precisely to the reserve about, or hostility towards, organised religion. In order that spirituality remains 'free' the common implication is that it must be an individual matter. The notion of life structure cannot, however, be very useful or ultimately transformative for individuals or society when it is related almost exclusively to the practice of isolated individuals.

I suggest, then, that there is room for exploration of how the experience of film-watching can be still more enriching and fruitful, individually and socially, through its comparison with religious practice. Practical ways in which this can occur are proposed in Chapter 7. To shift, however, from theology to spirituality, even though I think there is a sense in which the two are ultimately one (i.e. no thoughtless spirituality or soul-less theology is worth wasting time on), does at least leave my enquiry at a significant point. Exploration of film-watching has pressed in relation to each discipline – film studies and theology – the question how each might play its role in the search for an integrative approach to human living. In other words, how are theology's four dimensions (aesthetic, affective, cognitive and ethical) best handled within a structured approach to human living? What are religious believers likely to be weak on if they expect their religion to offer all to them, and if they are film-watchers, but expect little to come (save a good night out) from their cinema-going? In what ways is the 'religious' practice of cinema-going likely in the long-term to prove deficient for a regular viewer, for whom the Friday night out is a 'Sabbath', as far as drawing attention to the many dimensions of living is concerned? These are, I suggest, questions which the theology/religion-film dialogue could usefully fruitfully address.

Film-Watching as a Theological Habit: Locating This Book in Contemporary Discussion

The Christian church has been interested in film since its emergence. A mixture of caution, opposition and a desire to appropriate its potential has accompanied the rise of film since its appearance as a medium of communication in the late nineteenth century. What I have called throughout this book 'the theology/religion-film dialogue'[17] is more recent and can be dated from about 1970. Since then, a variety of forms of explicit recourse to film in theological discussion have been attempted.[18]

The 'theology/religion-film debate' is not, though, a debate internal to theology or religious studies. Indeed, one of the weaknesses of many contributions to the debate is the limited extent to which they have engaged with disciplines beyond religious studies and theology, not least with film studies. As this present study has shown, however, it is not film studies alone which must be drawn upon in order to do justice to what films actually do to people, and to what people do with films. This point has been emphasised by those who have sought to relate the 'theology/religion-film debate' to a variety of other disciplines, cultural studies in particular.[19] I

---

[17] For the remainder of this chapter I shall often refer to 'the theology/religion-film debate' simply because whether it is a 'dialogue' at all is a point of contention.

[18] These are, in turn, summarised in a variety of ways, e.g. by S. Nolan, 'The Books of the Films: Trends in Religious Film-Analysis', in *Literature and Theology* 12/1 (1998), 1–15 and Lyden, *Film as Religion*, ch. 1. R.K. Johnston, *Reel Spirituality: Theology and Film in Dialogue* (ch. 3) suggests there have been five 'theological approaches' dating back more than seventy-five years: avoidance, caution, dialogue, appropriation, and divine encounter, offering his own contribution in ch. 8 of that work, along two axes, the experiential and the critical.

[19] J.W. Martin and C.E. Ostwalt Jr (eds.), *Screening the Sacred: Religion, Myth and Ideology in Popular American Film*; M.R. Miles, *Seeing and Believing: Religion and Values in the Movies*.

conclude the main theoretical strand of this book by locating my proposal explicitly within recent contributions to the theology/religion-film debate, clarifying in so doing the inter-disciplinary nature of the enterprise of trying to understand how films work, especially as far as their reception is concerned. I shall locate my position in seven steps.

This present work will seem markedly different in approach from the earlier work on theology and film which I co-edited, and to which I contributed three chapters and a co-written response.[20] It remains, however, a contribution to a *dialogue* between theology and film even if the focus has shifted somewhat. I am yet more aware than I was in the mid–1990s of the radical extent to which all theology is inculturated. Even so, there is still a sense in which a theology is a communal attempt, by a religious tradition, to create a framework of thought and belief in relation to which that tradition's adherents live their lives. That framework is never 'pure'. But it is available for scrutiny, and seeks to be more than the mere self-expression of the experience of members of any particular religious tradition or community. Furthermore, the framework is intended as more than a value and belief system to which only some people (members of a given tradition or community) should attach significance. Theology is by definition not a sectarian activity. Theological frameworks make truth claims – claims to be saying something about how and what reality is – and as such invite consideration as to their truthfulness and usefulness by all human beings. Thus, though theological frameworks are never pure, they are to be detached from the circumstances of their origins and the concrete settings in which they continue to be held. Only in this way can the frameworks themselves be critically examined. Only in this way also can they fulfil the function of offering insight and critique of those who hold to the framework, and of the culture(s) in which adherents stand. As long as the vexing circularity of this relationship between theology and culture is recognised, I see no reason why the term 'dialogue' is inappropriate for the way theology works. I therefore also see no reason why 'dialogue' is not the best term to use for what goes on when theologians and religious studies specialists wrestle with the contemporary meanings and significance of film.[21]

In making this the first step of the clarification of my theoretical position, then – affirming the importance of dialogue – I distance

---

[20] Marsh and Ortiz (eds.), *Explorations*.

[21] In formal terms, then, this is no different to when theologians handle literature, fine art, architecture, sculpture or music which has no explicitly religious or theological content.

myself from a very recent contribution to the theology/religion-film debate, that of Gerard Loughlin. Loughlin's attempt, in *Alien Sex: The Body and Desire in Cinema and Theology*, to formulate what he calls a 'cinematic theology' seems to me to underplay the dialogical nature of what he undertakes.[22] Loughlin offers sophisticated and insightful readings of a number of films throughout his book. However, either he listens to them and learns from them in the process of offering his interpretations, or he presents his readings of film and his theological ideas in parallel, theology functioning as a kind of counter-assertion. In truth, both strategies appear to operate in the book at different times. But if he is doing the former, then the name 'dialogue' seems appropriate; if undertaking the latter, then what is the point of such extensive discussion of film?[23] Loughlin endeavours to accept theology's location in a complex culture and to respect the sensation of film-watching – endeavours which I wholeheartedly affirm. But I am not at all clear how his 'cinematic theology' works.[24] All theological exploration of supposedly non-theological cultural products (arts, film, media, sport) will run the risk of being charged with abuse and distortion. But without the acknowledgement of the dialogical nature of the exchange (there is an 'and' between theology and film), an appropriately theological and critical exploration simply cannot happen.

The second step of the clarification of my position needs to specify who the dialogue is between. Here I need to adapt my earlier work on the basis of its reception.[25] It is right to note that I have commended the value of conversation or negotiation between film (understood as a text) and theology (as a linguistic tradition). As the first step above indicated, I continue to believe this basic model to

---

[22] Loughlin, *Alien Sex*. For references to his contribution as 'cinematic theology' and 'cinematic body theology' see xx. Loughlin shows no awareness of the fact that an earlier contributor to the theology/religion-film debate, Neil Hurley, offered his own very different work, also in terms of a 'cinematic theology'. I am grateful to Steve Nolan for reminding me of this point.

[23] Except to 'set the cultural scene', perhaps.

[24] This does not, I stress, suggest that I have not found the book very valuable; on the contrary. Loughlin indicates a distancing from the dialogical approach to 'theology and film', xxix, n.64, where he states: 'Cinematic theology is not a dialogue, but a "becoming-other".'

[25] In what follows I am drawing especially on the interpretations stated or implied in Nolan, 'Books of the Films'; Plate, 'Religion/Literature/Film'; I. Wollaston, 'Theologizing Film', in *Reviews in Religion and Theology* 2 (May 1998), 5–10, Johnston, *Reel Spirituality*; and Lyden, *Film as Religion*.

be accurate and helpful. It does, however, need to be nuanced in a number of respects.

Steve Nolan has observed that all contributions which commend such a dialogue fall into the approach adopted by John R. May, and thus search for 'cinematic analogues' of religious and theological subject-matter.[26] His observation is telling, especially when turned into the form of critique: 'Consequently, his [i.e. May's] conception of film as "visual story" entirely misses the specific operations of film as experience.'[27] As this present study indicates, I have taken this criticism seriously. I have wanted to examine the film-watching experience more closely not merely to defend myself against the critique, but because it highlights what I believe to have been implicit in some of the contentions of earlier work.

It is striking that the opening sentence of *Explorations in Theology and Film* contains these words: '... the project began life with an overheard conversation in a pizza parlour on a Saturday evening in North London, England, in the late 1980s'.[28] That work, in other words, arose in part from the recognition that 'a film is always more than a film'. The film-watching experience includes many aspects both as a film is watched and afterwards. Recognition of cinematic analogues to theological subject-matter is *part* of that reflective process, but it is not all of what theology and religious studies can and need to do with film. Steve Nolan is thus half-right. To resist May's approach too strongly is to play down the symbolic worlds with which theology and work and in which Western culture is immersed. To accept Nolan's critique means being dissatisfied with a mere conversation between film and theology as 'texts'. This present study has sought to correct the 'over-textuality' of my earlier approach to dialogue, even whilst maintaining that dialogue remains an accurate image of what is going on.

But who is in dialogue? As this present study makes clear, it is not texts that talk but people. The notion of a dialogue between theology and film must therefore clarify who is talking. The academic conversation-partners involved in the theology/religion-film dialogue include: theologians speaking out of a specific religious tradition; religious studies scholars able to make comparative observations across religions; film studies specialists able to draw attention to how films work aesthetically; cultural analysts capable of commenting on film in a cultural context; sociologists who chart patterns of leisure consumption in society; and psychologists who

---

[26] Nolan 'New Religious Film Criticism', 171–2.
[27] Nolan 'New Religious Film Criticism', 171.
[28] Marsh and Ortiz (eds.), *Explorations*, 1.

observe the function of film upon a people's inner lives. Above all, however, the conversation must include those who actually watch films in the context for which films are usually intended: that of entertainment and leisure. Theology and film still function as 'texts'. There remain films and theological traditions that need interpreting. But the recognition of these many conversation-partners highlights the fact that it is people who do the interpreting, and that all interpretations of texts are brokered by mediators.

The third step of the clarification process draws on the distinction between theology and religion. One of the main confusions which has reigned in the theology/religion-film debate has been the meaning of these two, and related, key terms. From the 1970s onwards, references to 'theology' have often in practice meant 'religiosity', 'spirituality' or 'the spiritual', in so far as appeal was being made to general universal religious principles or values. Nolan's criticism of the May approach applies again here.[29] Both in the co-written final chapter of *Explorations in Theology and Film*, and in my Internet debate with John Lyden, however, I have sought to show that the challenge of post-liberalism to theology and religious studies at this point carries weight.[30] It is not necessary to agree with post-liberalism and conclude that theology is so bound to particular communities of faith that it is difficult for faith communities to talk to each other. It does, however, appear to me necessary to agree with post-liberals that more attention has to be taken of the particularity of religions, and of particular traditions within religions.

To talk, then, of 'theology and film' as if the dialogue entails the identification of universal religious principles in film is thus ultimately unhelpful because it is misleading. Such a view of the dialogue misconstrues how religions work and fails to respect films' integrity and the many dimensions of the film-watching experience. The dialogue between the many conversation-partners identified above will therefore need to respect the distinction between religion

---

[29] To his credit May himself has at least been consistent in referring to 'religion' or 'the religious', even if his interpretation of the two words is open to challenge.

[30] Marsh and Ortiz (eds.), *Explorations*, 246–7; J. Lyden, 'To Commend or to Critique?: The Question of Religion and Film Studies', in *Journal of Religion and Film* 1.2 (1997) < http://www.unomaha.edu/~wwwjrf/ tocommend.htm >; 'Continuing the Conversation: A Response to Clive Marsh', in *Journal of Religion and Film*, Reader Discussion, (1998) < http://www.unomaha.edu/~wwwjrf/disctopc.htm >; and *Film as Religion*, 254 n.67 and C. Marsh, 'Religion, Theology and Film in a Postmodern Age: A Response to John Lyden' in *Journal of Religion and Film* 2.1 (1998), < http://www.unomaha.edu/~wwwjrf/marshrel.htm >.

and theology so that the specificity of a religion, and thus the specificity of a theology worked out within that particular religion, are properly respected. A dialogue between theology and film therefore demands the question not only 'which film?' but also 'which, or whose, theology?'

In light of the third step, I come close to agreeing with the position articulated by John Lyden when he sees the 'religion-film dialogue as inter-religious dialogue'.[31] In order to respect the *de facto* function of film for many viewers and to acknowledge the embeddedness of religion within culture, Lyden draws on the theory and practice of dialogue between religions in order to clarify how the religious/theological function of film is best understood. In so far as the parallel Lyden draws fully respects film's own integrity, his strategy works. Film is acknowledged in all its 'otherness' as an important conversation-partner for theology.[32] The theological (as opposed simply to the comparatively religious) dimensions of the dialogue are also respected: there is truth at stake here as claims about reality are made.[33]

Lyden himself, however, slips rather too easily between theology and religion when he speaks of the 'dialogue between "religion" and "film" [as] … really just another form of interreligious dialogue' and claims that 'traditional religions might benefit from learning to listen to the religions of popular culture'.[34] In order to substantiate his case, Lyden is doing a number of things here. He is adopting a functional, sociologically-driven understanding of religion. Without this, he cannot call forms of popular culture 'religions'. I have taken a similar approach throughout this study in wanting to press the religion-like aspects of cinema-going as far as they will go, though, by contrast, I have not wanted to conclude that cinema-going *is* religion. Second, Lyden leaves no room for the practice of theology as a reflective discipline the task of which is actively to rework the symbol system within a given religious tradition. Without such an understanding, however, Lyden is back at the point where all theology and religion references are reduced to a generalised spirituality of universal principles. By contrast, I have worked throughout this study with an understanding of theology that acknowledges that specific beliefs and ideas, related to concrete religious practice, are being worked with. Theology is not reduced to a cognitive exercise alone when those beliefs are examined, critiqued and re-worked. Cinema-going, indeed, challenges

---

[31] Lyden, *Film as Religion*, ch. 5.
[32] Lyden, *Film as Religion*, 109–13.
[33] Lyden, *Film as Religion*, 113–4.
[34] Lyden, *Film as Religion*, 132.

theology's proneness to being over-cognitive. But the existence of specific beliefs, as opposed to general principles or values transcending all religions, has to be acknowledged, lest the integrity of theology itself is lost. Lyden, in short, does an excellent job of drawing out the necessary respect for the integrity of film in the theology/religion-film dialogue. But he does this, in my view, at cost to the integrity of theology.

The fourth step in the clarification of my position, then, is the maintenance of a clear position for theology's own integrity. Only in this way is true dialogue possible. In Lyden's terms, I end up an inclusivist.[35] I read film 'only through Christian categories or those of other traditional religions'.[36] My response is simple: I cannot do anything else (for I *am* a Christian). This does not mean that my beliefs are immovable. Nor does it mean that the tradition I inhabit, as a Christian believer, does not itself change around me. I have changed in my own beliefs, and it has changed over time. What happens when I watch films, as a Christian, is that I undergo an experience, the precise content of which I cannot control. And I am drawn into a complex conversation with many dialogue-partners the moment I begin to reflect on the content of the film and on the experience of watching it. I do not want to waste time arguing whether or not the experience of watching any particular film was a 'religious experience'. I am aware simply that the experience is always going to be religiously and theologically interesting, because it is through religious and theological lenses that I 'read' life. Theology itself develops, and its contents are not as clear-cut as may be first supposed. Theological engagement with the film-watching experience demands, in short, a very astute form of cultural theology indeed.

This brings me to the fifth step in my process of clarification. Here I take further the recognition of how immersed theology is in culture, in acknowledging that theology is inevitably a form of cultural studies. I make this fifth step, however, in two stages. By accepting the legitimacy of what Lyden is attempting, I accept that theology as a discipline has no *de facto* claim to be superior to any other in interpreting human experience. It has to fight its corner. In this sense, cultural studies subsumes all other disciplines in the humanities, for all human activity is culture. If, however, religion is

---

[35] Lyden's relates his discussion of the religion-film dialogue as inter-religious dialogue to the three possible positions commonly assumed to be tenable in inter-faith encounter: exclusivism, inclusivism and pluralism. Lyden's proposal in effect relates to the pluralist position though he does not fully explore the philosophical and theological implications that arise.
[36] Lyden, *Film as Religion*, 132.

part of human culture (as is clearly the case, despite what supporters of the secularisation thesis have sought to claim), then cultural studies must grant a place within its brief to religious studies and theological enquiry.

The theology/religion-film debate must therefore locate itself within a cultural studies framework, whilst seeking to maintain the integrity of religious studies and theology as disciplines. In this way, religious studies and theology may make a positive contribution to society and to cultural development not merely through their influence upon religious groups internally. As my discussion of Gilbey in Chapter 4 showed, this function and place for the theology/religion-film debate has an important public dimension. Unless this fifth step is taken, bad theology will be passed on throughout society without religious groups having much chance to do anything about it.

The sixth step of the clarification of my position takes a detour beyond the theology/religion-film debate as such and notes what is happening in film studies itself. The move from attention to films as texts to scrutiny of the reception of films coheres well with an interest in how films contribute to the construction and development of people's value-systems. In making the shift from examining only cinematic analogues to considering films alongside their impact upon audiences, I have found a number of allies.[37] Respect for actual audience responses to film may, of course, challenge my own personal theological interests. What if people do not generally share the perception that films sometimes evoke sentiments, arouse passions, or construct experiences of a 'religion-like' kind? What if films do not encourage viewers to ask big questions about life, and to reflect on the cognitive framework/s within which they live? What if film-going as a habit does not help people to structure their lives in a meaningful way, similar to the way a religion works? Such questions merely indicate that more enquiries are needed. But at least the allies in film studies, from whose work I have gained great profit, suggest that the pursuit of these lines of enquiry is not likely to be fruitless.

This brings me to my seventh and final step. Steve Nolan is indeed half-right: the search for cinematic analogues to theological themes has limited use. I disagree with him, however, about the way in which the theology/religion-film debate should look to film studies for help. In drawing on work in the reception of film, both in relation to cognitive psychology and on evidence of actual viewer

---

[37] These include Plantinga and Smith (eds.), *Passionate Views*;, Turner, *Film as Social Practice*; Barker, *From Antz to Titanic*; Jancovich and Faire, *Place of the Audience*.

response, I have sought to show that it is here where the future lies for theology and film. My difference from Nolan may be expressed this way: within the four dimensions of theology I identified earlier in this chapter, Nolan's preference for screen theory as theology's conversation-partner leads him to major on theology's aesthetic dimension. My interest in viewer response leads me to emphasise the emotional dimension. Both of us wish to do justice to what film studies can contribute to theology. Both of us remain interested also in theology's cognitive and ethical aspects. But the way we conduct our theological conversations with film reveals divergent focal points.[38]

An appropriate concrete next step for the theology/religion-film debate must therefore surely be to gather empirical data, similar to that being gathered for a variety of purposes within film studies,[39] about how films work. Data about the emotional, cognitive, aesthetic and ethical impact of film, and the location and function of film-watching within people's life-experience, would then facilitate the contemporary evaluation of film in relation to the concerns raised throughout this book. In this way, the notion of a dialogue between theology and film would open up into a rounded and informed conversation about the basis on which, and ways in which, critical reflection might happen in the context of ordinary living.

---

[38] It may also be possible to say that participants in the theology/religion-film debate who highlight aesthetics will be more drawn to art-house films, whilst those who are interested in films' emotional impact will work more with popular films (and vice versa in each case). How and why this should be so, and what this all means theologically, would also be worth scrutiny, but takes us well beyond what it is possible to examine here. These points also relate to the definition and function of 'kitsch' (see n.4–5 above).

[39] M.M. Davies and R. Pearson, 'Stardom and Distinction: Patrick Stewart as an Agent of Cultural Mobility – A Study of Theatre and Film Audiences in New York City', in T. Austin and M. Barker (eds.), *Contemporary Hollywood Stardom*, 167–86; Jancovich and Faire, *Place of the Audience*, both of which contain samples questionnaires indicating how relevant data has been collected.

A Film is Never Only a Film: Some Practical Conclusions

This concluding chapter brings together reflections on Chapters 1 to 6 and the case-studies (A-D). The basic point made by the book's structure is a simple one: theory gets interrupted. Life cannot be lived as a theory, not even when lived theologically. Though theology's cognitive aspect functions as a framework within which one chooses to live, neither this nor any other such framework (philosophical, political, ethical) is 'pure'. The practicalities of living intervene, and it is right and proper that they should. This reality of 'unsystematic living', as represented in the book's structure, confirms the importance of living as both embodied and influenced, even shaped, by both habits and interruptions, the precise content of which is not predictable or controllable.

This chapter therefore seeks to tease out consequences from the interplay of both strands in the book. What is to be made of the 'habit' of film-watching or cinema-going? What is theology's contemporary cultural role, for those inside and outside religions? What is the link, if any, between theology's cultural role and the practice of film-watching? I explore the consequences in the form of fourteen theses.

1. Life's disjointedness takes some handling.

We live in late-, or post-, modern times. Hallmarks of the cultural mood of our times have been identified already.[1] Finding a way of structuring one's life is thus arguably a harder task even than forty years ago. The demise of Christendom might well be a good thing, even for Christianityut, but there is little doubt that the new place in which people in the West find themselves is sometimes more unsettling than first thought.

In many ways, this book has been an exercise in acknowledging the impact of that cultural shift upon the practice of daily living.

---

[1] See section on 'The Critical Function of Theology' in Chapter 6 above.

Any study of an aspect of the interface between religion and culture has to attend to the present cultural climate. But it also needs to be practical ('OK, then, how will all this help me live my life better?'). This book has sought to be practical in two ways. It has sought to examine critically what is actually going on culturally in one area of artistic/popular cultural life: people are returning to the cinema in vast numbers, and the potential significance of this has been analysed. It has also sought to be realistic in its critical examination of theology's interaction with film. What points of connection *are* there between theology's work and what films are already doing to and for people?

The book has, however, examined a cultural form which may itself be open to the charge that it is merely an aspect of the postmodern mood. In addition to the hallmarks of contemporary culture already identified, the growing power of electronic media should be recognised too. The increase in cinema-going, when allied to the dominance of Hollywood, could thus be identified as no more than a form of controlled escape, and a trite one at that, from postmodern fragmentation. Life's disjointedness does take some handling: but it is handled through avoidance, the avoidance enabled by mass entertainment.

It would be hard to dispute that this avoidance will be happening for some film-watchers. I have tried in this book to suggest that it is not happening for all, and that it need not happen on the scale on which it may be occurring. I have sought to argue that theology is one of the necessary partners for those who take film seriously, and who want film's significant cultural function to be identified and developed. The handling of life's disjointedness – another way of saying 'living well today' – can therefore prove a creative task if the constructive, critical study of film and film-watching is undertaken alongside many other disciplines, theology included, as a 'life practice'.

The structure of this book has, however, demonstrated not only how film-watching can fulfil this function, but also how it has to operate in the midst of disjointedness. Film-watching does not always fit neatly into living, or address the issues and questions with which one might be dealing at the time. At this point, the habit of film-watching can learn from the practice of religion. Religious practices shape your life. They inform you gradually over time. Services of worship do not always 'work' in some utilitarian way. There is also a variety of practices entailed in being religious, for example, prayer, study, worship, charitable acts. All of these are entailed in a process of 'formation', in a positive, life-enhancing way. Film-watching can learn here too. A film is more than a film and merits thought and discussion. As a habit, as was noted in Chapter 1, film-going structures life. Film-watching can become still more if reflected upon in relation to other life practices.

Habitual, life-shaping practices thus themselves interrupt the flow of living. But certain, identified practices can themselves become a channel through which the disjointedness of life can be handled.

2. Spirituality is best understood as 'life structure'.

As soon as film-watching is seen not merely as entertainment, but as a 'life practice' around which so much else revolves, then its similarities to religious practice are clear. Seeing film-watching as a life practice, a discipline which one undertakes for many reasons and which has a broad impact on life, raised the question whether it helps shape a 'spirituality'. Perhaps it even *is* a spirituality for the most regular of cinema-goers. What, though, is meant by this?

It helps to see film-watching as a spiritual discipline in two respects. Regular film-watching shapes a pattern of living. It also forms a major channel through which thoughts, feelings, and aesthetic and moral sensibilities are stimulated and developed. In this way, then, it proves a major way in which personal development happens. It could be said that it pertains to the 'inner life'. But this may prejudge what people mean by 'spirituality', and demand more, ideologically, than some contemporary interpreters would be willing to concede. For perhaps there is no 'inner life' as such. Perhaps all really is 'surface'. Perhaps the whole of life really is relationships (apart, that is, from the chemical functions of the body). Perhaps all 'selves' are socially constructed. 'Spirituality', if used at all as a term, is thus the name given to a set of practices in which the self is constructed.

From most religious and theological perspectives, of course, there will not be much support for negation of the inner life. Religious perspectives struggle in the opposite direction: against overemphasis upon the inner life. 'Spirituality' too easily becomes attention to the spirit or soul, at cost to the body. Examination of the practice of film-watching is enlightening here in a number of respects. First, film-watching accentuates the fact that whether explicitly religious or not, all human beings find some ritual practices in relation to which they structure their lives. Second, it reminds religions that the most meaningful practices are those which requires attention to many dimensions of living: emotional, cognitive, aesthetic and ethical. Third, it pays more attention than some contemporary forms of religion – certainly some forms of contemporary Christianity – to the importance of embodied ritual experience. Finally, it raises the question of the importance of a social dimension to ritual experience. None of these four insights is incompatible with a concern for the 'inner life', in the sense in which theology would normally use the term. But none inevitably requires it either. Both for this reason and because 'spirituality' is simply used in so many different ways in contemporary culture, I suggest that seeing film-watching as spiritual discipline can mean no more, in fact, than that it helps people structure their lives.

3. Spirituality without theology is vacuous.

Spirituality is of itself, however, not enough. To say that you have structured your life in some way, and found some way of handling life's disjointedness, says nothing about on what basis you may have done this. It is for this reason that the four dimensions of theology (cognitive, affective, aesthetic and ethical) were highlighted. It is here, in relation to spirituality, where their importance becomes clear. For a person to say that they 'have a spirituality' indicates at the very least that they have a life structure, whether or not the value-system(s) in relation to which such a structure is formed are always clear. 'Having a spirituality' may mean more: that a person is clear that they undertake work on their 'inner life'. But even here, the cognitive framework within which a person seeks to develop their inner life, or through which they wish to see their inner life developed, may not be explicit. It is at this point that the cognitive aspect of the task of theology needs to be prominent. A spirituality cannot function unless it relates to an ideological (here, theological) framework. Where a spirituality does not make this explicit, then hidden ideological frameworks operate. In the present climate, therefore, many contemporary 'spiritualities' are allied to the worship of the body, as they focus on physical fitness.

A theological approach to spirituality requires attention to all dimensions of living including the cognitive, and thus of the 'life structure' which attention to spirituality produces. What will this mean? To give examples based on main chapters from this book: it matters what salvation means, and how such salvation is to be received (Chapter 3); it matters what views of God and God's action people hold (Chapter 4). 'Salvation' can be shaped in meaning in all sorts of directions. But at some point, the precise content of the term invites an interpreter to ask: 'but why "salvation" as opposed just to "feeling better" or "being released"?' At that point, the theological-ideological framework within a religious tradition which speaks of salvation, redemption or liberation is required as a conversation partner in order for the concept to be grasped. Again, the images of God purveyed inside and outside of religion matter culturally.

Without critical examination of such images, cultures operate with assumed images of God. In our contemporary supposedly secular culture, images of God are often presented by those ill-equipped to do so. This was the focal point of my discussion of Gilbey in Chapter 4. Theological reflection is thus needed at the heart of culture even when it is assumed by some cultural critics that religion is a marginal matter.

Spirituality without theology is thus in danger of being vacuous. And as a consequence of a failure to address theological concerns in relation to spirituality, Western culture's handling of spirituality becomes deficient.

4. The practice of theology makes integrated living easier.

A theologically-informed spirituality therefore has more opportunity to function as a comprehensive life structure than one which leaves any of the four aspects unexplored. Two questions arise, however. Why theology? And will any theology do?

Theology is not, of course, the only possible cognitively-interested conversation partner for the practice of film-watching. Philosophical and political frameworks also shape human living. They can shape human living equally significantly as religion and theology. I have to admit at this point that what I have constructed is a largely *formal* argument for theology's relevance to film studies. I have not written a book of Christian apologetics which seeks to argue Christian theology's primary claim to be the most significant conversation-partner. That was not my purpose. I have, however, sought to show the legitimacy of theology as a conversation-partner.

Will *any* theology therefore do? Does it matter whether the theology with which one converses with film is Hindu, Jewish, Christian or Muslim? Even in Christian terms, does it matter whether the theology is radical, liberal, conservative, or post-liberal? Does it matter whether the theology is offered by Roman Catholics, Baptists, Methodists or Anglicans? Again, in a formal sense, it does not matter at all. The fact is that films *are* watched within diverse religious (and other) frameworks. Religious traditions, theological persuasions and confessional allegiances all contribute to the construction of particular cognitive frameworks within which people watch films. Diverse theologies do come into play. At its richest, then, theological reception of, and conversation with, film would entail discussion of film within an explicit awareness of diverse possible responses. Discussion of *The Shawshank Redemption* invites the reflections of many religious traditions each handling their own diverse theologies of salvation.

This does not, however, turn theology into a matter of indifference. To say that any theology *can* be a conversation partner in a formal sense does not render all theologies of equal weight. To ask the question how one decides between theologies (across and within religious traditions) is, however, to ask two further questions. On the one hand, how are religions to be 'graded'? On the other, how, within a religious tradition are the respective merits of different theological persuasions to be evaluated? Such questions takes us well beyond the parameters of this book, but must not ultimately be dodged. On the contrary, this study of the contemporary significance of film-watching suggests that film could be one medium through which some forms of interfaith encounter may be fostered, and some forms of discussion about the cultural role of religion may be developed.

5. To see film-watching as a spiritual discipline does not spoil the watching of a film.

It may, though, be argued that despite appearances to the contrary I have revealed myself as a true Puritan. Have I not located the practice of film-watching so firmly within an educative, character-building context that I have ended up arguing against the sheet enjoyment of watching a film? Have I not argued the entertainment element away altogether? I do not believe so. Robert Johnston writes:

> To reflect analytically and constructively on a movie's meaning is to treat the film with the seriousness its creators intend. If the movie is meant to be simply entertaining, mere escapist fare, theological conversation is of course pointless. But so too is any film criticism. What we have is the equivalent of pulp fiction or dime store romances. Just as there are bad novels and trite paintings, so there are confused or hackneyed movies. But for any film that seeks to connect with its viewers with regard to the human condition, or to offer a vision of transcendence whether human or divine, theological criticism is both appropriate and even necessary.[2]

This is a telling quotation which enables me to get to the heart of my enquiry. It appears in Johnston's section headed 'The Critical Axis'. (He has already considered 'The Experiential Axis' arguing, as I do, that films first need to be *experienced* before theological reflection can do its work.) Johnston is not, in other words, suggesting that any and every film seen provides material for theological reflection. Theology has a critical role to play. I wholeheartedly agree. My problem is with the full implications of what his approach entails.

---

[2] Johnston, *Reel Spirituality*, 162–3.

First, he puts too much weight on directors' intentions. He implies that only if directors have serious intentions can serious consequences be drawn. It is, however, possible that a director's primary intent to entertain may nevertheless produce a film that does more than this. It is even possible that a bad film may produce a level of serious reflection which proves highly instructive. Second, Johnston does not indicate by what criteria good and trite films can be thus labelled. The charge of 'mere escapist fare' is as easily made about films as it is about different forms of worship by those who prefer different forms, or who do not worship at all. Beginning from what films do to people, or make people feel (in terms of laughter, reflection, feeling joyful or sad) may produce quite different results from those Johnston supposes. Third, as with most analogical approaches to film, the good and bad films are likely to be identified upfront in terms of their theological usefulness on grounds of theme.

By contrast, I do not want to have my film-watching controlled quite as neatly. I do not usually watch what the film critics suggest to me, via their reviews, will be trash. But sometimes I do go to films that are not recommended. Usually the film critics are right, though not always. I want to be able to watch a Jim Carrey film without the expectation, in every case, that it will be an edifying experience. I want to watch, from time to time, a horror film, in order to be shocked and scared, in a protected environment. Even if my emotions are not wholly 'real', for a short time they are real enough. Through such experiences I may learn more than expected, and be provoked to think about things I had not anticipated. But sometimes I am not looking for such an experience and do not therefore judge films accordingly. I am not, however, expecting to pigeonhole films in any simple way. It is for this reason that a 'frothy' film like *Shirley Valentine* should be allowed to do more than its critics, and theologians, often expect.

Theological engagement with film thus has to be cautious lest it restrict the possibilities of what films can achieve, and take away the sheer potential for enjoyment of the film-watching experience. On the contrary, theological engagement should be able to become one of the means by which film-watching may be enhanced, through being a resource through which the experience of film-watching can be processed.

6. A film theatre is never only a film theatre.

If a film is never only a film, then a film theatre is never only a film theatre. As the multiplexes now show quite clearly, they are entertainment centres, with bars and cafés to hand. Smaller independent film-theatres show, in addition, their awareness of their educative role through their provision of study days, themed screenings, and lecture series. It is worth exploring further what is known already to happen, and to suggest what might yet be possible.

At multiplexes there are sometimes special 'adults only' screenings of even 12 and 12A-rated films. Particular auditoria have licensed bars attached so that viewers can sit, drink and talk in comfort before and after a film. A social practice is thus created which is already much more than the viewing of the film. It would not be too much for any particular group (education class, church, film club, book group) to enter into a partnership with a multiplex on a regular basis to use such facilities for special screenings, with built-in discussion.

Educational events offered by smaller film-theatres include, for example, explorations of 'what it means to be human', death and afterlife, and war, as handled by recent film. Sometimes these are study days on which two or three major films on a topic are shown in a single day, with brief, oral introductions. One film theatre known to me offered a philosophy study day around three films.[3] Theological discussion could easily be stimulated in a similar format.

One striking development in Britain in recent years has been the alliances between national newspapers and cinema chains, offering free preview tickets to forthcoming films. Though this naturally figures as part of a programme of advanced publicity for a newly-released film, one cannot but notice that many such screenings happen on Sunday mornings. Gatherings of enthusiastic cinema-goers (who do not even have to pay for the privilege) thus occur at many venues around the country on a regular basis. These bodies of people then, in turn, pass on their evaluations of, and reflections on, films viewed to many others (to those of us who then have to pay!). It is an example of effective marketing and wise use of premises – the cinemas are filled at times when they would otherwise not be. But it is also a good example of how to gather a group of informed enthusiasts to do a task (the critique and, hopefully, commendation of a film) merely by virtue of asking them to do what they already enjoy doing.

7. New ways of 'being church' will include finding ways of respecting people's cinema-going habits.

In Christianity today there is much talk of 'new ways of being church'. Such conversations recognise the limited capacity of 'old'

---

[3] And philosophy through film textbooks now exist; see e.g. M.M. Litch, *Philosophy Through Film.*

(and often still current) ways of being church to prove attractive to large numbers of people. It is difficult to determine whether this is due to widespread loss of belief, or more due to the cultural alienness of much ecclesiastical practice. For some Christians, the notion of bringing a concern about decline in churchgoing alongside recognition of the popularity of film would signal the beginning of the end. New ways of being church would seem inevitably to turn churches more towards the entertainment industry.

As I have sought to show throughout this book, however, my own purpose in exploring film as a theological resource is not to rescue churches as we know them. Though I have examined the overlaps and distinctions between cinema-going and worshipping, my purpose is not to establish mere relevance in order to get people back into church. I am, of course, keenly interested to develop the life of the Christian Church. I do not, however, think that mere attention to film-watching practices will achieve this. Rather, my purpose has been to note what films do in fact do to people and what people do in fact do with films. Only then is it worth reflecting on how churches might be affected by resulting insights. And such reflections need to be made alongside wider recognitions of the role that theology might play within culture.

Examples of what may be achievable in terms of communal theological reflection, in relation to film, extend the examples provided in the previous section. If multiplexes and film theatres could prove to be more than mere 'houses of illusion' through the opportunities they offer for reflection, then churches can do likewise. Three examples suggest themselves. Again, these are not merely theoretical. They are already beginning to happen.

Groups of Christians are attending films together and then discussing the experience. In this way, Christian groups are acknowledging the fact that many Christians are already keen cinema-goers. Groups are created across age bands, and a social activity becomes something more: a stimulus for reflection and theological exploration. When undertaken in Christian groups, the reflection may, of course, be less wide-ranging than would be undertaken in groups of people of different religious traditions or none. But such Christian groups are not required to limit their explorations to what, in a film, is compatible with Christian faith. Exploration of a film's content, and of a film-watching experience, can stretch contemporary Christians in their reception, appropriation and rethinking of their belief structure.

Church buildings are becoming places where film discussion groups meet. Here, the distinction between church as people and church as building is important. Admittedly, for some, even the task of entering a church building is difficult. For those with no or bad experience of Christianity, the assumption that all religious faith is about brainwashing can prevent their taking the risk of joining groups which happen to meet on church premises. Where churches are recognised as cultural centres (and their use as community and education centres is becoming more and more common), then churches can function not only as bases for groups, but also as initiative-takers in stimulating reflection on film. A challenge for churches (understood as groups of Christian people) is whether they can be active in the promotion of life-enhancing film-discussion groups. Is it possible for Christians at local level to promote groups which do not require Christian commitment, but which genuinely enable people who have an interest in film to discuss what they have viewed? Such groups could be pioneering in interfaith encounter, in practical philosophical exploration, and in personal and cultural development. Such groups would come under the banner of 'lifelong learning' in the broadest sense of that term, whether or not they are examples of formal education.

The challenge to churches can be further extended to consider ways in which they may set up formal partnerships with film-theatres. One Roman Catholic Church known to me has a link with a nearby film theatre, as a result of which, on a regular basis, those attending evening Mass move from the church to the theatre to watch a film together. It is seen as part of their communal life as a worshipping community.

All of these examples begin to stretch an understanding of how churches function and how the practice of 'being church' interweaves with the practice of film-watching. They indicate that the communities within which theological exploration can happen are more flexible than may be sometimes supposed. None of the above is a formal educational setting. Two relate to identifiable church groups, but only the third correlates directly with a single worshipping community. Though it may, therefore, be quite correct to stress the close relationship between the doing of theology and the worshipping practice of the church, theological reflection can also begin and be conducted beyond churches. This broader cultural exploration of theology must not be overlooked. In examining how films function culturally, this broader exploration is exposed, and its importance highlighted. It is a practical consequence of the academic insight that the theology/religion-film dialogue is best located within cultural studies.

8. It is better to go to the cinema than to watch a film at home.

Religious rituals can be individual or social. But religious affiliation entails some kind of belonging to a community, however tenuous that communal link might be. It is not possible to 'inhabit' a religious tradition without some sense of attachment to (even dependence on) a body of people which carries the tradition along with you. Cinema-going can be solitary, but usually is not. There is rarely a sense in which attenders of a film-showing at a multiplex constitute a 'community' in which people know each other. Talk of a 'community of cinema-goers' is thus rather farfetched. At most it could apply to members of a film club or society. But I have already stressed in Chapter 2 above that the sense of 'communal belonging' in religious worship can sometimes be overplayed. Despite the relative anonymity of cinema-going, the communal dimension of watching a film in public, as opposed to the privacy of a home, must be emphasised. Why is this?

First, more happens when you watch a film at the cinema. The reactions of other people inform our viewing. Second, the viewer's attentiveness is assisted. It is much harder to walk out of a cinema than to switch off a video. Third, cinema-going with friends means that there are people on hand to discuss the film with immediately. Reflection is prompted as soon as a film finishes. Because this occurs, it is also more likely that immediate emotions are reported and worked upon than if a film is watched at home. Fourth, because more happens, viewers have more to discuss. It is more likely, then, that more than the content of the film can feature in post-film discussion.

The distinction between public and private film-watching, then, has some of the same socio-psychological dynamics as the distinction between public and private spirituality. There is more to respond to from the public aspect of each. Admittedly, in the case of either film-watching or religious devotion, individual attentiveness can be enhanced in private watching or worship. But the fact that more happens when people meet should scarcely cause surprise: a communal experience is itself more than the sum of the experience of individuals.

There is, however, one aspect of the preference for cinema-going which should not be overlooked by those of us who want to draw a parallel between cinema-going and religious practice: cinema-going costs money. Home viewing is cheap by comparison. Stressing the value of public film viewing thus implies that viewers have enough disposable income to participate in a certain style of life. Religious devotion need entail no direct economic outlay. Cinema-going requires financial participation in an industry. Again, the distinction can be overdrawn. Religious commitment quickly demands of people a careful look at how they spend money. Cinema-going could be woven into life as an entertaining pastime, but one taken as seriously as, say, education. It may thus be seen as both a welcome release from work or routine living, but also be considered money well spent. But this economic aspect of film-watching does indicate a point at which cinema-going and social religious practice can be sharply distinguished.

9. Film critics and film studies lecturers need to be better informed about religion and theology.

One clear consequence of the enquiry conducted in this book is a challenge to film critics and film studies lecturers to be better informed about religion and theology. In the same way that the knowledge of art critics about the religious subject-matter of the work they study is sometimes found wanting, so also the limitations of film critics in their attentiveness to religious subject matter, or to the potential of understanding film in theological perspective, can easily be seen.

With film there is a dimension beyond that of static art. The power of the moving image and the communal aspect of viewing create extra dynamics to the interpretative task. As this book has sought to show, if such dynamics do not *require* religious or theological interpretation, they do more than merely *permit* such interpretation. The *de facto* function of film in contemporary Western culture at least suggests to interpreters operating within a cultural studies perspective that religion should not be overlooked when the reception of films is studied.

10. Theologians and religious studies lecturers need to be better informed about popular culture.

Similarly, a challenge is issued to theologians and religious studies lecturers to be more attentive to popular culture. An interest in popular culture tends, in religious studies and theology, to be the preserve of a few. At most, as we have seen, it receives attention within the domain of practical theology. When theology takes in the arts, popular culture usually continues to lose out. I recall, in the course of a single conversation some years ago with a distinguished Cambridge theologian, watching his eyes glaze over when I spoke of my work on film, only for him to reconnect with the conversation when I referred to a second project on Christology. This often seems to be the experience of people who try to keep a foot in both camps: trying to maintain a serious interest in popular culture for serious theological purposes is not always met with seriousness in theology.

In Christian understanding this will not do for three theological reasons. The doctrine of creation underpins an appropriate attentiveness to everything creative fashioned by human hands. The doctrine of incarnation demands respect for materiality, and urges embodied beings to acknowledge their enfleshment: no total spiritualisation of human experience is thus possible in theological understanding. The doctrine of the Spirit serves as a reminder of the constantly creative Spirit of God at work within human creativity. This three-sided approach to respect for human artistic endeavour does not justify every cultural product as an equally valid or equally revelatory work of God. But it does invite caution before popular culture is devalued, or too easily labelled as trite, or 'kitsch'. Theologians and religious studies lecturers may thus need to pay attention to more than merely popular religious culture in order to undertake their work adequately in the present.

11. Religion could itself be revitalised through critical film-watching. Film-watching could be enhanced by relating to critical theology.

I come to my boldest claims yet. Religions and film-watching could both be revitalised through reference to the critical function of the other. By this I simply mean that at a time when the purpose and usefulness of religion is often unclear to many people, the bringing closer together in mutual critical scrutiny of the two practices of film-watching and religious devotion has the chance of informing each. To those who like film, but are baffled by religious practice, the critical comparison of the two practices invites closer scrutiny of the rewards of attentiveness to the film-watching process. To the religious who are puzzled at how and why people waste so much time staring at a screen, the many-dimensional impact of a multi-sensual experience serves as a jolt reminding them of a persuasive power that religions have often lost.

I stress again: in no way is the dialogical enquiry conducted throughout this book undertaken merely in order to bolster religions generally, or Christianity in particular. Serious engagement with the practice of film-watching and the content of films studied should not, in fact, leave Christianity unchanged. If a dialogue is real then film does not simply become a disguised medium for transmitting an already-known 'message'. Christianity is far from contentless: it brings a cognitive content and a set of existing practices to the dialogue. Its capacity to evolve is, however, clear. It has often changed throughout history, even whilst remaining identifiably 'Christian'. This means that the interaction between film-watching and Christian thought and practice in the present is but a recent episode in the development of Christianity, as it seeks to fashion an appropriately cultural theology. Furthermore, placing the emphasis upon the *practice of film-watching* as well as the *content of film* reminds cultural interpreters that theology relates to religious practice and is not merely about ideas and beliefs.

On the other hand, religious interpreters have a role to play not merely as critics of particular films. The four aspects of theology's task may all be drawn upon in the critical assessment of film's cultural function. I am not at all sure that theologian Graham Ward will be sympathetic to my line of argument throughout this book (too accommodationist, I imagine). But he would surely concur with the notion that theology retains an important critical function. If theological reflection does not do this then it will not actually be fulfilling its crucial role in society. In the present context, theologies must find out how to be appropriately assertive and challenging, without being arrogant or bombastic.

12. Emotionally conscious theology is not only for charismatics.

One clear offshoot of this study is the insight that theology deals with the affective life, and that interaction with film stimulates theology to address this in unexpected ways. Exploration of the impact of sentimentality in film invites deeper exploration of a theology of sentiment. If I am right to draw attention in particular to the way in which theology contributes to the structuring of the emotional life, then a cultural responsibility of theology becomes clear. In the context of enabling people to reflect on films and film-watching, viewers are being helped in their emotional development. Insofar, then, as theological engagement with film enables an appropriate cognitive structuring of the emotions of the viewer as disclosed by the film-watching experience, theology is contributing to emotional health.

Theology's contribution to reflection upon the film-watching experience does, however, also function critically of the notion that the arousal of emotion is inevitably of itself a good thing. The location of such arousal within a broader framework of interpretation and meaning (i.e. within theology's four-dimensional task) provides opportunity for reflection upon a film's effects. The emotions aroused in the film-watching experience may not be 'controlled', 'contained' or 'restricted' by such a process. Nor may they even be fully understood. The reflection process simply prevents the arousal of emotion being lost, proving quietly destructive (if negative emotions have been aroused by a film) or insufficiently valued (if positive).

The interaction between film and theology thus challenges theology to respect fully its affective dimension. It also urges that theology does not siphon off its concern for the affective to be located only in worship or only in the worship conducted by Christians of a particular theological persuasion, for example, charismatics. Theology is thus reminded that there are other ways in which theology's affective dimension can be enjoyed, grasped and addressed, and that such emotionally conscious theology is not always simply emotionally driven, narcissistic or autobiographical.

13. The question of what and who 'God' is remains vital throughout.

A critical reader of a draft of this manuscript commented: 'by far the biggest thing that your book does to me is make me question the whole God issue'. This is as it should be. I have sought to keep 'the whole God issue' alive throughout the book. I have sought not to assume a particular belief about God on the part of readers whilst suggesting that the enduring fascination of religious practices needs still to be explored in our supposedly secular age. I believe the durability (and ultimately the relevance) of those practices depends on there being a reality – God – to which theistic religious practices point. I have not, however, argued that case in this book. Instead, I have sought to explore one example of religion-like practices into which some of the concerns with which religion continues to deal have been displaced. The 'whole God issue' is more important than the question of particular religions. But I have expressed the view throughout that the God issue cannot be handled without reference to particular traditions. The practical impact of film-watching, then, can itself raise 'the whole God issue'. It is up to interpreters of films and their impact to ensure that the issue is appropriately addressed.

14. The only theology worth bothering with is a culturally informed and culture-critical theology.

The final heading functions as a summary not only of this last chapter but also of the whole book: the only theology worth bothering with is a culturally informed and culture-critical theology. Attention to film and the practice of film-watching accentuate these mutually critical aspects of theology's task: how culture critiques theology, and how theology critiques culture.[4] Theology must be constantly critiqued by cultural products all around it, for it too is located within culture (understood as human society) and many cultures (in the sense of particular communities of practice and discourse). It must also critique what it sees around it, for it has a part to play in cultural development, deriving from the traditions, experiences and reflections of particular religious traditions.

Christian theologies thus wrestle with Christian sources and resources in the task of the criticism of culture and its products. But they do so not from a position of simple superiority. Christian claims to speak on God's behalf need to be muted, even whilst they claim to be based on revelation, for all religion involves projection and social self-interest as well as the proven usefulness of an established tradition of thought. Self-criticism can, however, prove debilitating, and churches can be harder on themselves than they sometimes need to be, especially at a time of numerical decline in the West. The particular 'God tradition' which Christianity carries with it has more to be said for it than much Western culture currently allows. If this needs to be put in the context of what it can offer with regard to the enrichment of life, then so be it. I am not sure that accentuating this positive, this-worldly, world-affirming aspect of religion is necessarily to sell out to consumer culture. But to develop that argument would demand a different book.

Critique nevertheless remains part of theology's task. I have sought to show in this book what kind of critique will prove culturally beneficial, as well as what theology itself may gain from film. If the book encourages more of this, I shall be more than pleased.

---

[4] Or, more accurately, how cultures critique theologies and how theologies critique cultures, for there is much diversity.

Bibliography

Argyle. M., *The Social Psychology of Leisure* (London: Penguin Books, 1996)

Arthur, C., 'Review of "Explorations in Theology and Film"', in *Media Development* 2 (1998), 59–60

Astley, J., *Ordinary Theology: Looking, Listening and Learning in Theology* (Aldershot/Burlington, VT: Ashgate, 2002)

Austin, T and M. Barker (eds.), *Contemporary Hollywood Stardom* (London: Arnold, 2003)

Baker, J. and D. Gay, *Alternative Worship* (London: SPCK, 2003)

Barker, M. with T. Austin, *From Antz to Titanic: Reinventing Film Analysis* (London/Sterling, VA: Pluto Press, 2000)

Beaudoin, T., *Virtual Faith: The Irreverent Spiritual Quest of Generation X* (San Francisco: Jossey-Bass, 1998)

Bergan, R., *The Coen Brothers* (London: Orion Media, 2000)

Blandford S., B.G. Grant and J. Hillier, *The Film Studies Dictionary* (London: Arnold, 2001)

Blum C., 'Sentiment', in J. Yolton, R. Porter, P. Rogers and M. Stafford (eds.), *The Blackwell Companion to the Enlightenment* (Oxford/Cambridge, MA: Blackwell, 1991), 487–8

Bordwell, D., *Making Meaning: Rhetoric and Inference in the Interpretation of Cinema* (Cambridge, MA: Harvard University Press, 1989)

Brock, R.N., *Journeys By Heart* (New York: Crossroad, 1991)

Brock, R.N. and R.A. Parker, *Proverbs of Ashes* (Boston: Beacon Press, 2001)

Brown, C., *The Death of Christian Britain* (London and New York: Routledge, 2001)

Brown, F.B., *Good Taste, Bad Taste, and Christian Taste: Aesthetics in Religious Life* (New York: Oxford University Press, 2000)

Brown, J.C. and C.R. Bohn (eds.), *Christianity, Patriarchy and Abuse* (New York: The Pilgrim Press, 1989)

Bruce, S., *Religion in Modern Britain* (Oxford: Oxford University Press, 1995)

Bruce, S., *Religion in the Modern World* (Oxford: Oxford University Press, 1996)

Bruce, S., 'The Problems of a Liberal Religion: A Sociologist's View', in M.D. Chapman (ed.), *The Future of Liberal Theology* (Aldershot and Burlington, VT: Ashgate, 2000), 221–41

Butler, R., 'A Night at the Pictures in 1994', in *Independent on Sunday*, 16 December 1994, 18–19

Carroll, N., 'Film, Emotion, and Genre', in C. Plantinga, C. and G.M. Smith (eds.), *Passionate Views: Film, Cognition, and Emotion* (Baltimore and London: The Johns Hopkins University Press, 1999), 21–47

Cheshire, E. and J. Ashbrook, *Joel and Ethan Coen* (Harpenden: Pocket Essentials, 2002)

Clements, K., *Friedrich Schleiermacher: Pioneer of Modern Theology* (London: Collins, 1987)

Clinebell, H., *Basic Types of Pastoral Care and Counselling: Resources for the Ministry of Healing and Growth* (London: SCM Press, 1984)

Coates, P., *Cinema, Religion and the Romantic Legacy* (Aldershot/Burlington, VT: Ashgate, 2003)

Crichton, J.D., 'A Theology of Worship' in C. Jones, G. Wainwright and E. Yarnold (eds.), *The Study of Liturgy* (London: SPCK, 1978), 1–29

Darabont, F., *The Shawshank Redemption: The Shooting Script* (London: Nick Hern Books, 1996)

Davie, G., *Religion in Britain Since 1945: Believing Without Belonging* (Oxford: Blackwell, 1994)

Davie, G., *Religion in Modern Europe* (Oxford: Oxford University Press, 2000)

Davies, M.M. and R. Pearson, 'Stardom and Distinction: Patrick Stewart as an Agent of Cultural Mobility – A Study of Theatre and Film Audiences in New York City', in T. Austin and M. Barker (eds.), *Contemporary Hollywood Stardom* (London: Arnold, 2003), 167–86

Deacy, C., *Screen Christologies: Redemption and the Medium of Film* (Cardiff: University of Wales Press, 2001)

Dougan, A., *Robin Williams* (London: Orion, 1998)

Drane. J.W., 'Celebrity-Centric Religion', in C. Partridge (ed.), *Dictionary of Contemporary Religion in the Western World* (Leicester/Downers Grove: Inter-Varsity Press/InterVarsity Press, 2002), 185–8

Eitzen, D., 'The Emotional Basis of Film Comedy' in C. Plantinga and G.M. Smith (eds.), *Passionate Views: Film, Cognition and Emotion* (Baltimore/London: Johns Hopkins University Press, 1999), 84–99

Evans, J., *The Penguin TV Companion* (2nd edn.; London: Penguin Books, 2003)

Fane-Saunders, K. (ed.), *Radio Times Guide to Films* (2nd edn.; London: BBC Worldwide, 2001)

Frijda, N., A.S.R. Manstead and S. Ben (eds.), *Emotions and Beliefs: How Feelings Influence Thoughts* (Cambridge: Cambridge University Press, 2000)

Frijda, N. and B. Mesquita, 'Beliefs through emotions', in N. Frijda, A.S.R. Manstead and S. Ben (eds.), *Emotions and Beliefs: How Feelings Influence Thoughts* (Cambridge: Cambridge University Press, 2000), 45–77

Frye, N., *The Great Code: The Bible and Literature* (Harcourt Brace Jovanovich: New York, 1981)

Gaut, B., 'Identification and Emotion in Narrative Film', in C. Plantinga and G.M. Smith (eds.), *Passionate Views: Film, Cognition and Emotion* (Baltimore/London: Johns Hopkins University Press, 1999), 200–16

Gilbey, R., 'I've got that sinking feeling', in *The Independent*, 23 January 1998

Gledhill, R., 'Trite films fail to show true love, says bishop', in *The Times*, 29 April 2000

Graham, E., *Representations of the post/human: Monsters, aliens and others in popular culture* (Manchester: Manchester University Press, 2002)

Gray, D., 'Worship' in A. Hastings, A. Mason and H. Pyper (eds.), *The Oxford Companion to Christian Thought* (Oxford: Oxford University Press, 2000), 762–4

Gregory, R.L. (ed.), *The Oxford Companion to the Mind* (Oxford: Oxford University Press, 1987)

Grodal, T., *Moving Pictures: A New Theory of Film Genres, Feelings and Cognition* (Oxford: Clarendon Press, 1997)

Guner, F., 'The artist ascending' in *The Independent*, 14 January 2003, Arts Section, 14–15

Hastings, A., *A History of English Christianity 1920–1985* (London: Collins, 1986; expanded edn. *A History of English Christianity 1920– 2000*; London: SCM Press, 2001)

Herrmann, J., *Sinnmaschine Kino: Sinndeutung und Religion im populären Film* (Gütersloh: Christian Kaiser/Gütersloher Verlagshaus, 2001)

Hess, M., 'Practising Attention in Media Culture' in J. Mitchell and S. Marriage (eds.), *Meditating Religion: Conversations in Media, Religion and Culture* (London/New York: Continuum, 2003), 133–42

Hollows, J. and M. Jancovich (ed.), *Approaches to Popular Film* (Manchester: Manchester University Press, 1995)

Hornby, N., *Fever Pitch* (London: Gollancz, 1992)

Hornby, N., *How to Be Good* (London: Viking, 2001)

Hughes, G., *Worship as Meaning: A Liturgical Theology for Late Modernity* (Cambridge: Cambridge University Press, 2003)

Jancovich, M. and Faire L. with S. Stubbings, *The Place of the Audience: Cultural Geographies of Film Consumption* (London: BFI Publishing, 2003)

Jasper, D., 'On Systematizing the Unsystematic', in C. Marsh and G. Ortiz (eds.), *Explorations in Theology and Film* (Oxford: Blackwell, 1997), 235–44

Jenkins, P., *The Next Christendom: The Coming of Global Christianity* (New York: Oxford University Press, 2002)

John, J. and M. Stibbe, *The Big Picture: Finding the Spiritual Message in Movies* (Bletchley: Authentic, 2002)

Johnston, R.K., *Reel Spirituality: Theology and Film in Dialogue* (Grand Rapids: Baker Academic, 2000)

Kermode, M., *The Shawshank Redemption* (London: BFI Publishing, 2003)

Kirsner, I., *Erlösung im Film: Praktisch-theologische Analysen und Interpretation* (Stuttgart/Berlin/Cologne: Kohlhammer, 1996)

Litch, M.M., *Philosophy Through Film* (New York/London: Routledge, 2002)

Loughlin, G., *Alien Sex: The Body and Desire in Cinema and Theology* (Oxford: Blackwell, 2004)

Lubin, D., *Titanic* (London: BFI Publishing, 1999)

Lupton, D., *The Emotional Self: A Sociocultural Exploration* (London, Thousand Oaks/New Delhi: Sage, 1998)

Lyden, J., 'To Commend or to Critique?: The Question of Religion and Film Studies', in *Journal of Religion and Film* 1.2 (1997) < http://www.unomaha.edu/~wwwjrf/tocommend.htm >

Lyden, J., 'Continuing the Conversation: A Response to Clive Marsh', in *Journal of Religion and Film*, Reader Discussion, (1998) < http://www.unomaha.edu/~wwwjrf/disctopc.htm >

Lyden, J., *Film as Religion: Myths, Morals and Rituals* (New York and London: New York University Press, 2003)

Lynch, G., *After Religion: 'Generation X' and the Search for Meaning* (London: Darton Longman & Todd, 2002)

Maher, I., *Faith and Film: Close Encounters of an Evangelistic Kind* (Cambridge: Grove Books, 2002)

Marsh, C., 'Film and Theologies of Culture' in C. Marsh and G. Ortiz (eds.), *Explorations in Theology and Film* (Oxford: Blackwell, 1997), 21–34

Marsh, C., 'The Spirituality of *Shirley Valentine*' in C. Marsh and G. Ortiz (eds.), *Explorations in Theology and Film* (Oxford: Blackwell, 1997), 193–205

Marsh, C., 'Did You Say "Grace"?: Eating in Community in *Babette's Feast*', in C. Marsh and G. Ortiz (eds.), *Explorations in Theology and Film* (Oxford: Blackwell, 1997), 207–18

Marsh, C., 'Religion, Theology and Film in a Postmodern Age: A Response to John Lyden' in *Journal of Religion and Film* 2.1 (1998), < http://www.unomaha.edu/~wwwjrf/marshrel.htm >

Marsh, C., *Christianity in a Post-Atheist Age* (London: SCM Press, 2002)

Marsh, C., 'Religion and the Arts' in C. Partridge (ed.), *Dictionary of Contemporary Religion in the Western World* (Leicester/Downers Grove: Inter-Varsity Press/InterVarsity Press, 2002), 65–8

Marsh, C., 'Sex, Shopping, and Other Weighty Theological Matters (1)', *Epworth Review* 31/1 (Jan. 2004), 23–30

Marsh, C., 'Sex, Shopping, and Other Weighty Theological Matters (2)', *Epworth Review* 31/2 (April 2004)

Marsh, C. and G. Ortiz (eds.), *Explorations in Theology and Film* (Oxford: Blackwell, 1997)

Martin, J.W. and C.E. Ostwalt Jr. (eds.), *Screening the Sacred: Religion, Myth and Ideology in Popular American Film* (Boulder: Westview Press, 1995)

Marwick, A., *The Sixties: Cultural Revolution in Britain, France, Italy, and the United States, c.1958–c.1974* (Oxford: Oxford University Press, 1998)

McDannell, C. and B. Lang, *Heaven: A History* (London/New Haven: Yale University Press, 1988)

McGrath, A. (ed.), *The Blackwell Encyclopedia of Modern Christian Thought* (Oxford/Cambridge, MA: Blackwell, 1993)

Miles, M.R., *Seeing and Believing: Religion and Values in the Movies* (Boston: Beacon Press, 1996)

Mitchell, J., 'Emerging Conversations in the Study of Media, Religion and Culture', in J. Mitchell and S. Marriage (eds.), *Meditating Religion: Conversations in Media, Religion and Culture* (London/New York: Continuum, 2003), 337–50

Mitchell, J. and S. Marriage (eds.), *Meditating Religion: Conversations in Media, Religion and Culture* (London/New York: Continuum, 2003)

Mottram, J., *The Coen Brothers: The Life of the Mind* (London: Batsford, 2000)

Nolan, S., 'The Books of the Films: Trends in Religious Film-Analysis', in *Literature and Theology* 12/1 (1998), 1–15

Nolan, S., 'Looking Sharp', in *Third Way* (December 1998), 23–6

Nolan, S., 'Carpe Phallum: (Male) Salvation Meta-Narrative and The Renewal' in M.A. Hayes, W. Porter and D. Tombs eds. *Religion and Sexuality* (Sheffield: Sheffield Academic Press, 1998), 285–311

Nolan, S., 'Review of *Screen Christologies*, Christopher Deacy', in *RRT* 9 (2002), 460–5

Nolan, S., 'Towards a New Religious Film Criticism: Using Film to Understand Religious Identity Rather than Locate Cinematic Analogue', in J. Mitchell and S. Marriage (eds.), *Meditating Religion: Conversations in Media, Religion and Culture* (London/New York: Continuum, 2003), 169–78

Nolan, S., 'Representing Realities: Theorizing Reality in Liturgy and Film', in *Worship* (2003), 149–72

Otto, R., *The Idea of the Holy* (Oxford: Oxford University Press, 1950; [German original: 1917])

Peterson, G.R., *Minding God: Theology and the Cognitive Sciences* (Minneapolis: Fortress Press, 2003)

Plantinga, C. and G.M. Smith (eds.), *Passionate Views: Film, Cognition, and Emotion* (Baltimore/London: The Johns Hopkins University Press, 1999)

Plate, B., 'Religion/Literature/Film: Towards a Religious Visuality of Film', in *Literature and Theology* 12 (1998), 16–38

Postman, N., *Amusing Ourselves to Death: Public Discourse in the Age of Show Business* (New York/London: Penguin/Methuen, 1985/1987)

Redeker, M., *Schleiermacher: Life and Thought* (Philadelphia: Fortress Press, 1973)

Riches, J., *The Bible: A Very Short Introduction* (Oxford: Oxford University Press, 2000)

Rojek, C., *Celebrity* (London: Reaktion Books, 2001)

Romanowski, W.D., *Eyes Wide Open: Looking for God in Popular Culture* (Grand Rapids: Brazos Press, 2001)

Schleiermacher, F.D.E., *The Christian Faith* (Edinburgh: T&T Clark, 1928; [German original; 2nd edn.; 1830])

Schleiermacher, F.D.E., *On Religion: Speeches to Its Cultured Despisers* (New York: Harper Torchbooks, 1958; [German original: 3rd edn. 1822])

Schmucler, H., 'The scandal of aestheticising horror: thoughts on *Schindler's List*', in *Media Development* 1 (1995), 26–7

Stone, B.P., *Faith and Film: Theological Themes at the Cinema* (St Louis: Chalice Press, 2000)

Tan, E.S., *Emotion and the Structure of Narrative Film: Film as an Emotion Machine* (Mahwah: Erlbaum, 1996)

Tan, E.S. and Frijda, N., 'Sentiment in Film Viewing' in C. Plantinga, C. and G.M. Smith (eds.), *Passionate Views: Film, Cognition, and Emotion* (Baltimore/London: The Johns Hopkins University Press, 1999), 48–64

Thrower, J., *Religion: The Classical Theories* (Edinburgh: Edinburgh University Press, 1999)

Tracy, D., *The Analogical Imagination: Christian Theology and the Culture of Pluralism* (London: SCM Press, 1981)

Turner, G., *Film as Social Practice* (3rd edn.; London and New York: Routledge, 1999)

Vaux, S.A., *Finding Meaning at the Movies* (Nashville: Abingdon Press, 1999)

Wakefield, G., 'Spirituality, Forms of', in A. Hastings, A. Mason and H. Pyper (eds.), *The Oxford Companion to Christian Thought* (Oxford: Oxford University Press, 2000), 685–6

Walker, J. (ed.), *Halliwell's Film and Video Guide 2004* (London: HarperCollins, 2003)

Walker, J. (ed.), *Who's Who in the Movies* (3rd edn.; London: HarperCollins, 2003)

Walsh, J., *Are You Talking To Me?: A Life Through the Movies* (London: HarperCollins, 2003)

Ward, G., *True Religion* (Oxford: Blackwell, 2003)

Watts, F., *Theology and Psychology* (Aldershot/Burlington, VT: Ashgate, 2002)

Watts, F. and M. Williams, *The Psychology of Religious Knowing* (Cambridge: Cambridge University Press, 1988)

Weaver, J.D., *The Nonviolent Atonement* (Grand Rapids: Eerdmans, 2001)

Williams, M.E., 'Cinema', in A. Hastings, A. Mason and H. Pyper (eds.), *The Oxford Companion to Christian Thought* (Oxford: Oxford University Press, 2000), 121–2

Winter, R., *Still Bored in a Culture of Entertainment* (Downers Grove: InterVarsity Press, 2002)

Wollaston, I., 'Theologizing Film', in *Reviews in Religion and Theology* 2 (May 1998), 5–10

Wright, A., *Why Bother with Theology?* (London: Darton, Longman & Todd, 2002)

Film Index

General Index